DATE DUE

THE PRIMA DONNA

Da Capo Press Music Reprint Series

MUSIC EDITOR
BEA FRIEDLAND
Ph.D., City University of New York

This title was recommended for Da Capo reprint by
Frank D'Accone, *University of California at Los Angeles*

THE PRIMA DONNA

Her History and Surroundings from the Seventeenth to
the Nineteenth Century

BY

H. SUTHERLAND EDWARDS

IN TWO VOLUMES

VOL. I

DA CAPO PRESS · NEW YORK · 1978

Library of Congress Cataloging in Publication Data

Edwards, Henry Sutherland, 1828-1906.
    The prima donna.

    (Da Capo Press music reprint series)
    Reprint of the 1888 ed. published by Remington, London.
    1. Singers—Biography. 2. Opera. I. Title.
ML400.E28 1978   782.1'092'2 [B]   77-17875
ISBN 0-306-77536-0

This Da Capo Press edition of *The Prima Donna, Volume I*
is an unabridged republication of the first edition
published in London in 1888.

Published by Da Capo Press, Inc.
A Subsidiary of Plenum Publishing Corporation
227 West 17th Street, New York, N.Y. 10011

THE PRIMA DONNA

THE PRIMA DONNA

Her History and Surroundings from the Seventeenth to the Nineteenth Century

BY

H SUTHERLAND EDWARDS

IN TWO VOLUMES

VOL I

London

REMINGTON AND CO PUBLISHERS

HENRIETTA STREET COVENT GARDEN

1888

Preposterous ass! that never read so far
To know the cause why music was ordained!
Was it not to refresh the mind of man
After his studies or his usual pain?

Taming of the Shrew.

                    Shining ones who thronged
Eastward and westward making bright the night.

Light of Asia.

Soprano, mezzo, even the contralto
Wished him five fathoms under the Rialto.

Beppo.

CONTENTS.

CHAPTER I.

THIS most fortunate among women was unknown
to antiquity ; she belongs essentially to modern
times. Like the actress, to whom she is generally
superior by her indispensable artistic training,
though often inferior in native wit, she is a product
of the last two hundred years. In 1687 the only
stage favourite known up to that time in England
was Nell Gwyn, who died that year. A great
Italian singer, Adriana Baroni, was known to a few
by the Latin verses which Milton addressed to her :
" Ad Leonoram Romæ canentem." But though
Adriana Baroni was famous in Italy, and though
Cardinal Mazarin took her with him as a member of
the select company which he formed with the view
of establishing Italian opera in France, she never
visited our country; and no singer of the first
distinction was heard in England until Margarita
l'Epine arrived here in 1692.

In our earliest operatic representations the prima donna counted, indeed, for very little. Who, in the present day, knows or cares to know that when, during the Commonwealth, in the year 1656, *The Siege of Rhodes* was produced at Sir William Davenant's theatre, with music by Matthew Lock, Henry Lawes, and others, the principal female part was taken by Mrs. Coleman? Yet Mrs. Coleman was the first dramatic singer—the first prima donna, that is to say—who was heard in England; as she was the first actress, moreover, who appeared on the English stage.

A marked distinction was made at that time between plays that were acted and plays that were sung. The former were looked upon as offensive by reason of the frequent coarseness of the spoken dialogue; whereas the latter (as an edict on the subject put it), being in an " unknown tongue," could not corrupt the morals of the people. The " unknown tongue " was simply music. The first opera that appeared in England was, in fact, described as " a representation by the art of perspective in scenes, and the story sung in recitative music." No one, even in those Puritan times, seems to have seen anything to object to in the appearance of a woman on the public stage. The scandal caused a few years afterwards, under the Restoration, by the performance of some actresses imported from France, was probably due to scandalous demeanour on their part; perhaps, also, in some measure to the mere fact of their being French. They can scarcely have been actresses in the ordinary sense of the word; for in what piece could they have played with a chance of making themselves understood? Apparently they were dancers.

Mrs. Coleman was, in any case, our first English prima donna, as Nell Gwyn was our first popular actress. But the former lady seems to have confined herself to singing the music assigned to her, some of which was the composition of Dr. Coleman, her husband. The latter, by her liveliness, her beauty, her graceful audacity, and by the influence she exercised over King Charles II. (or "Charles the Third," as she preferred to call him, in allusion to his being her third lover of that name), became a personage of European celebrity; so that if Dryden had never written plays, and, better still, epilogues for her, and if Pepys had never made entries in his diary on the subject of " witty, pretty Nell," and the pleasure which, even in presence of his wife, he took in embracing her ("especially the kissing of Nell"), we should still have known her from the Grammont memoirs, and from the admirable account given of her in connection with her aristocratic rival Mdlle. de Quérouailles, by Madame de Sévigné. In spite of her three Charleses, Nell Gwyn possessed good qualities; and such was the belief both of the eminent ecclesiastic who preached her funeral sermon and of Queen Mary, who being told, in malice, what Dr. (afterwards Archbishop) Tennison had dared to do, replied that " this was to her a proof that the poor woman had died penitent."

Whether Nell Gwyn was the daughter of a captain in the army, as she was inclined to believe, or of a fruit-seller in Covent Garden, as her enemies asserted, she had, in any case, been allowed to grow up among evil surroundings. Considering the uncertainty of the evidence, and in view of the laws of heredity, it is difficult to admit that the graceful Nell can have been of low origin by both parents. It is easy to guess the truth in this matter. But, however that may be, the poor girl had nothing to guide her in life but her own natural tendencies, which, fortunately, were in the main good. The successful singers of that period were, on the other hand, women of good breeding and of the highest education. The before-mentioned Adriana Baroni was the daughter of a singer almost equally celebrated, Leonora Baroni. One of the most distinguished of her companions in the art was Francesca Caccini, daughter of the composer of the same name, who, in association with another composer, Peri, and with Rinuccini as librettist, produced *Dafne ;* which passes for the earliest complete opera, with airs, recitatives, choruses, and instrumental preludes. But there were in those days no newspapers to record the performances and sound the praises of the Baronis and the Caccinis; who are consequently little to us now beyond mere names.

We know, however, from a work of the time how the singers of the seventeenth century were trained. It can be shown, too, from many sources in what esteem they were held, and often not for their musical attainments alone. It was at the beginning of this century that they took the name of "virtuosi," to distinguish themselves from ordinary actors. Ferri (to turn for one moment from female to male singers) was looked upon as so distinguished a personage that when Queen Christina of Sweden wished to hear him she sent a vessel of war to bring him to Stockholm. Stradella (regarded as the only singer who, by the exercise of his art, had saved his life until the legend on the subject was destroyed by Mr. Mazzucato, in Grove's " Dictionary of Music ") composed an opera whose transcendent merits caused him to be proclaimed by authority " the first Apollo of Music." " Senza contrasto il primo Apollo della musica," said the official stamp imprinted on the published score. Atto, who, with Leonora Baroni, was a member of the company selected by Mazarin to be taken to Paris (1645), had apartments assigned to him in the Cardinal's Palace, and was afterwards sent by Mazarin on a political mission to the Court of Bavaria.

As to the course of study, both for men and

women, Bontempi, in his " Historia Musica," speaking of a school established by Mazzocchi, at Rome, in 1620, describes it as follows: " The pupils had to give up one hour every day to the singing of difficult passages till they were well acquainted with them; another to the practice of the shake; another to feats of agility [vocal agility, that is to say] ; another to the study of literature; another to vocal exercises under the direction of a master, and before a looking glass, so that they might be certain they were making no disagreeable movement of the muscles of the face, of the forehead, of the eyes, or of the mouth." So much for the occupation of the morning. In the afternoon half an hour was devoted to the theory of singing ; another half hour to counterpoint; an hour to hearing the rules of composition, and putting them in practice ; and the rest of the day to practising the harpsichord and to the composition of some psalm, motet, canzonet, or any other piece according to the scholar's own ideas. Such were the ordinary exercises of the school on days when scholars did not leave the house. If they went out they often walked towards Monte Nuovo, and sang where they could hear the echo of their notes, so that each might judge by the response as to the justness of his execution. They, moreover, performed at all the musical solemnities of the Roman churches ; following and observing with attention the manner and style of a number of great singers who lived under the pontificate of Urban VIII., so that they could afterwards render an account of their observations to the master, who, the better to impress the result of these studies on the minds of his pupils, added whatever remarks and cautions he thought neces- sary.

None of the great singers of the seventeenth century came to England. Italian music had not yet been introduced, and it was the strange custom in those distant days to offer to the English music-loving public operas written in the English language. Not that the composers were necessarily English. After the restoration, Lawes and Lock were succeeded and partially displaced by Cambert, who, in combination with the Abbé Perrin, had founded the " Académie Royale de Musique," as from the first the French opera-house was called ; but who, soon afterwards, was ejected from his post through the intrigues of Lulli. Cambert's operas, composed to French words, were translated before being presented to English audiences ; and Grabut, who had accompanied Cambert to London, and who remained after Cambert's death, composed music expressly for Dryden's *Albion and Albanius,* 1685. Then for a few years Dryden found an associate in one of the most English of English composers, though as Purcell in a dedication says himself of contemporary music in England : " 'Tis now learning Italian, which is its best master, and studying a little of the French air, to give it somewhat more of gaiety and fashion."

A few years before the death of Purcell, which took place in 1695, London received a visit from Margarita de l'Epine, the first Italian singer whose presence in England has been recorded. She could not for the best reasons sing to us on her arrival in Italian opera. But she sang with the greatest success Italian airs; and she remained here so long that she was able to take part in establishing Italian opera in England, when, during the early part of the eighteenth century, that form of entertainment was at last introduced.

A so-called Italian opera by an Englishman named Clayton, who had composed his work in Italy, was produced at Drury Lane in 1705; the same Clayton who afterwards set to music Addison's *Rosamond*, and who, as representing native talent, joined two foreigners, named Nicolo Haym and Charles Dieupart, in an attempt to put down the foreigner Handel. *Arsinoe*, as Clayton's lamentable work was called, could not, being composed to an Anglicized libretto, suit Margarita de l'Epine, who sang only in Italian; and the part for the prima donna was assigned to Margarita's English rival, Mrs. Tofts. For from the very beginning of operatic representations in England, no prima donna of mark has ever been without a

rival; nor has either of the rivals failed to find
support from a sworn body of partisans among the
public.

Mrs. Tofts, then, was the first prima donna who
sang on the English stage in what was professedly
an Italian opera.

Arsinoe was followed by *Camilla*, the second
opera in the Italian style that was produced in England. *Camilla*, however, was really in the Italian
style, though it was found impossible to play it in
Italian. Nor could it be given throughout in
English. So when it was brought out at the Opera
House erected by Sir John Vanburgh on the
site now occupied by Her Majesty's Theatre an
arrangement was come to by which the Italians,
with Signor Valentini at their head, were to sing
their parts in Italian, while Mrs. Tofts, the English
prima donna, was to sing hers in her native tongue.
Camilla was the work of Marco Antonio
Buononcini, brother of the Buononcini whose
name was to be handed down to us less through
his music than by a too famous epigram. This
epigram, by the way, though not the work of Swift
is quite worthy of him, both by its merits and its
defects. Compare with it his entry on the subject
of Margarita de l'Epine in the " Journal to Stella,"
as to his hearing " Margarita and her sister, and
another drab, and a parcel of fiddlers at Windsor."

This entry was made in 1711, a year after the

production of Buononcini's *Almahide*, memorable
as the first Italian opera produced on our stage
in which the parts were sung throughout in the
Italian language. This gave Margarita a chance ;
and it was she, in fact, who undertook, in *Almahide*, the part of the prima donna. The public,
according to Addison, had by this time got tired of
understanding only half the opera, and were pleased
to find it unintelligible from beginning to end.
" Future historians," he wrote at another time,
" will record that at the beginning of the eighteenth
century the English were so well acquainted with
Italian as to have their plays habitually performed
in that language." There was at least, however,
one vocalist in the cast of *Almahide* who apparently could make nothing of the tongue in which
he was condemned to sing. This was an Englishman named Lawrence, of whom, in proposing a
Greek opera, Addison wrote that he could " learn
the language as well as he had learnt Italian in a
fortnight's time."

In connection with Margarita de l'Epine and Mrs.
Tofts, the two leading prime donne of the first
decade of the eighteenth century in England, must
be mentioned a charming English singer named
Campion, who died, much regretted, in 1705, at the
age of 18.

In 1714 Anastasia Robinson came on the scene,

to disappear from Italian opera and from the stage generally in 1724.

This takes us up to and beyond the time of Durastanti, and brings us to the period of the two formidable rivals, each formidable to the other, Cuzzoni and Faustina; and it will be interesting to see how Durastanti is eclipsed by Cuzzoni, and Cuzzoni again by Faustina, while Faustina will in her turn have to give way to Mingotti.

Meanwhile, Italian opera having temporarily gone under, English opera—"the Beggars' Opera," that is to say—has temporarily come up, and with it the charming Lavinia Fenton, who soon, however, disappears in company with a duke.

This incident, taken in connection with similar ones in the lives of Anastasia Robinson and of Miss Campion, suggests the inspiriting thought that at the feet of the prima donna lies a path that may lead to the most dazzling altitudes. An Englishman may gain entry to the House of Lords by way of the House of Commons, the army, or the bar; or, if he does not mind being only a life-peer, through the Church. But for an Englishwoman who has a career to make, the only road to the peerage is by way of the stage.

That is the great lesson taught by the history of the prima donna, at least of the English prima donna, during the eighteenth century. How it happened that Anastasia Robinson became a countess, and Lavinia Fenton a duchess, while poor Miss Campion would also, beyond doubt, have become a duchess had she not died so young, will be shown in future chapters. Even the unfortunate Mrs. Tofts, before her insanity declared itself, married a consul, who, as his post was Venice, still at that time an important city, was doubtless a Consul-general.

The Italian singers, on the other hand, threw themselves away in the most reckless style; marrying people of their own profession, from interested composers and speculative managers to musical agents and theatrical loungers. One of the most famous, too, of these foolish virgins fell into dire distress, so that it was only by petty handiwork that she was able, in her last days, to keep body and soul together. This also will be shown.

CHAPTER II.

A CENTURY and a half ago, as now, the English public was accused of preferring foreign to native talent; which, as Italy was at that time beyond question the first musical country in Europe, it may well, so far as Italians were concerned, have done. Yet the three English singers who graced the early part of the eighteenth century, Mrs. Tofts, Anastasia Robinson, and Lavinia Fenton, were certainly appreciated. Carey, however, among others, did not think so; for in doggerel not unworthy of the bard to whom we owe the words of "God save the Queen"* he wrote, in reference to Anastasia Robinson's alleged superiority to Cuzzoni —

> With better voice, and fifty times her skill,
> Poor Robinson is always treated ill;
> But such is the good nature of the town,
> 'Tis now the mode to cry the English down.

* The words sung by Carey on a memorable occasion, and said to have been written by him, were translated from a Latin anthem, beginning " Salvum fac Dominum," which had been sung in James the Second's chapel; to what music has not been recorded, though the rhythm of the verses is sufficiently suggestive.

The English, in any case, began by crying the foreigners down; and even such men of wit as the writers in the *Spectator* used systematically to ridicule Handel and Buononcini to the greater glory of the British impostor named Clayton. Addison must have been sincere in admiring the man—who probably had more talent for talking about music than for composing it—or he would not have written for him the libretto of *Rosamond.* Clayton is only known in the present day as the composer of what Mr. W. A. Barrett has called " the worst opera ever written ; " though it may be doubted whether the *Arsinoe* of the same master was not quite as bad as the work to which, in the way of badness, Mr. Barrett accords the preference. Strange that, so few years after the death of Purcell, the English should have recognized as their leading composer—at least, as regards prominence of position—one who, while trading on the accident of having been born in England, borrowed his airs from Italy, and received help in arranging them for the orchestra from a French violinist named Dieupart and a German violoncellist named Haym !

Clayton's prejudice against Italian composers did not extend to Italian singers. But the services of the only eminent Italian singer at that time in England could not be turned to account in *Arsinoe;* since that opera, though composed to an Italian libretto, was to be performed in English, a language which Margarita de l'Epine, in spite of her twelve years' residence in England, had not yet mastered.

Arsinoe was announced in the *Daily Courant* as "a new opera after the Italian manner, all sung, being set by Master Clayton, with dances and singing before and after the opera by Signora Margarita F. de l'Epine." The wording of this notification might well suggest that Margarita de l'Epine was at once a singer and a dancer. She was only a vocalist, however, and not even, at this time, a dramatic vocalist; for no opera had yet been produced in which a part could be assigned to her. The musical plays of an earlier period were no longer performed. But the operas of Italy had not yet been introduced; and the Italian vocalist whom the English had now adopted as their own had, since her first appearance, confined herself to singing at concerts. Her original intention in coming to England seems to have been to make merely a passing visit. She gave a farewell concert the very year of her arrival, 1692; and, anticipating one of the fashions of a later age, continued to give farewell concerts until, at last she settled quietly down among her newly-found admirers and went on singing to them for a period of thirty-four years. Probably no Italian prima donna ever enjoyed such a long career as this first specimen of the class known in England.

It has already been set forth that after *Arsinoe,*

an Italian opera sung in English, came *Camilla*, an Italian opera sung half in English, half in Italian; which was followed by *Almahide*, sung entirely in Italian. From this time forward Italian singers, even to the present day (or let us say until a year or two ago), were to have a fine time in England. But in the earliest period of Italian opera, as established in this country, the principal female parts were assigned to two " leading ladies," of whom one was English-born, while the other, though Italian by birth, was virtually naturalized in England and ended by marrying an Englishman. The two great rivals, Mrs. Tofts and Margarita de l'Epine, were succeeded, moreover, by an English-woman, Anastasia Robinson; who obtained as great a success as either of her predecessors, and who, in spite of Carey's clumsy lines, was highly appreciated. She, indeed, for some years reigned supreme on the operatic stage.

Margarita de l'Epine's long career includes the whole of this operatic period. She had been singing for eighteen years in England when in 1710 Buononcini's *Almahide*, in which the principal female part had been allotted to her, was brought out; and she continued singing after Mrs. Tofts had retired through madness, and Anastasia Robinson through marriage. She liked England so well that quite in her early days she sent to Italy for her younger sister, who had been trained for the operatic stage, but who, soon after her arrival in London, married a Colonel in the English army and renounced all idea of a musical career.

Even the ill-favoured Margarita de l'Epine seems to have had a chance of marrying a British noble-man, as her contemporaries Anastasia Robinson and Lavinia Fenton were both to do. It is certain that the Earl of Nottingham fell desperately in love with her, and a clever woman would have known how to turn his passion to account. On one occasion he is said to have thrown himself at the feet of "Greber's Peg," as Margarita was sometimes called in reference to her having been brought to England by a young music-master named Greber; and the incident inspired Rowe with the following epigram, more coarse than witty :—

> Did not base Greber's Peg inflame
> The sober Earl of Nottingham,
> Of sober sire descended ;
> That, careless of his soul and fame,
> To play-houses he nightly came,
> And left church undefended ?

Margarita, when she at last determined to abandon the stage—a resolution which must have been powerfully aided by the striking success of Cuzzoni about that time—gave her hand to a scientific man, Dr. Pepusch, who was philosopher enough to set no particular store on youth and beauty. He knew that his wife was plain, and used playfully to call her "Hecate," a doubtful piece of pleasantry which she seems to have taken in good part. He must have known also that she had stored up a small fortune. It was only ten thousand pounds; but money was of more value a hundred and sixty years ago than now, and vocalists of less.

Margarita de l'Epine retired and got married the very year in which Anastasia Robinson did the same. Her ten thousand pounds enabled Dr. Pepusch not only to pursue his experiments with ease, but also, as Dr. Barry puts it, "to live in a style of elegancy which, until the time of his marriage, he had been a stranger to."

If Margarita was notorious for her ugliness, even when, as a young woman, she first came out, Mrs. Tofts was renowned for her beauty.

Mrs. Tofts sang in public for only a few years. We first hear of her as a concert-singer in 1703, before the introduction of opera (properly so called) into England. In 1705 she appeared in Clayton's too famous *Arsinoe*, and soon afterwards in the *Camilla* of Marco Antonio Buononcini, brother of Handel's future rival—the before-mentioned half English, half Italian work. The music of her voice, combined with the fascination of her personal appearance, had its effect even upon Swift, to whom Margarita de l'Epine was only a "drab." Mrs. Tofts seems, however, to have possessed a reputation for other qualities which can scarcely be commended; though it may be

doubted whether, as possessed by Mrs. Tofts, they
justified our sledge-hammer satirist in addressing to
her these lines :—

> So bright is thy beauty, so charming thy song,
> That it draws both the beasts, and their Orpheus along ;
> But such is thy av'rice and such is thy pride,
> That the beasts must have starved, and the poet have died.

At the beginning of the eighteenth century the
title of " Mrs." was sometimes given to single
women, and there is nothing to show that " Mrs."
Tofts was ever married until after her retirement
from the stage she became the wife of Mr. Joseph
Smith, British Consul at Venice. Colley Cibber
praises her for her " exquisitely sweet silver tone,"
and for a " peculiar rapid swiftness of the throat."
She does not appear to have been more than six
years before the public, for she is not to be heard
of before the year 1703, and she withdrew from the
stage finally in 1709. Her rivalry with Margarita
de l'Epine is the first of the kind on record, and as
such may be worth a passing notice. No one seems
to have wished to enjoy the talent of both. Those
who admired the one would decry the other; and
when, as sometimes happened, they sang together
at the same concert (they seldom took part in the
same opera), there were disturbances in the
audience department, so that neither could be
heard. On one occasion, now historic, Margarita
de l'Epine, singing at Drury Lane Theatre, was
hissed, hooted, and at last made a target for oranges

thrown at her by some woman, who could not but be regarded as one of Mrs. Tofts' partisans.

The thrower of oranges was arrested, much scandal was caused, and on the 4th of February, 1704, the following statement on the subject was published in the *Daily Courant* :—

" Ann Barwick having occasioned a disturbance at the Theatre Royal on Saturday last, the 5th of February, and being therefore taken into custody, Mrs. Tofts, in vindication of her innocence, sent a letter to Mr. Rich, master of the said theatre, which is as followeth :—

" Sir,

" I was very much surprised when I was informed that Ann Barwick, who was lately my servant, had committed a rudeness last night at the playhouse, by the throwing of oranges and hissing, when Mrs. l'Epine, the Italian gentlewoman sang. [Margarita de l'Epine, then, was also called ' Mrs.'] I hope no one will think it was in the least with my privity, as I assure you it was not. I abhor such practices ; and I hope you will cause her to be prosecuted, that she may be punished as she deserves.

" I am, sir, your humble servant,

" KATHERINE TOFTS."

Ann Barwick's hatred of her late mistress's rival had indeed been expressed in a most objectionable manner. Her zeal had carried her too far. But, considering her position in life, her conduct had been scarcely worse than that of many other partisans.

The London public must, at the beginning of the eighteenth century, have been strongly predisposed towards operatic music; in which what chiefly pleased it was apparently the singing, since the pieces, to judge by the accounts handed down to us, were entirely wanting in dramatic merit, while the music fitted to them, instead of being written expressly for the words, had for the most part been borrowed from various inappropriate sources. One opera, *Pyrrhus and Demetrius* (the music arranged by Nicolo Haym from the original of Adriano Morelli), was played at increased prices for no less than thirty nights. The success was apparently due to the strength of the cast, which included Margarita de l'Epine and Mrs. Tofts in the leading parts, a mysterious " Baroness " and the favourite male singer named Valentini in the minor ones.

This was the last work in which the beautiful Katherine Tofts appeared. Soon afterwards a terrible misfortune befell her. Her brain gave way, and the enemies of Italian Opera pretended that she had become demented through extravagant joy at her own stage triumphs. " This lady," wrote Steele in the *Tatler*, " entered so thoroughly into the great characters she acted that when she had finished her part she could not think of retrenching

her equipage, but would appear at her own lodging
with the same magnificence that she did upon the
stage. This greatness of soul has reduced that
unhappy princess to an involuntary retirement,
where she now passes her time amid the woods and
forests thinking of the crowns and sceptres she had
lost, ever humming in her solitude —

> " I was born of royal race,
> Yet must wander in disgrace."

But for fear of being overheard, and her quality
known, she usually sings it in Italian —

> " Nacqui al regno, nacqui al trono,
> E pur sono
> Sventatura."

This verse is from one of the airs which the unfortunate prima donna had sung with striking
success in the opera of *Camilla.*

Mrs. Tofts recovered from her painful malady,
but did not return to the stage. It has already
been said that she became the wife of a rich connoisseur, Mr. Joseph Smith, who soon after his
marriage received the appointment of British
Consul at Venice, where he and his beautiful but
still somewhat deranged wife lived for many years.

Margarita de l'Epine had now the public entirely
to herself. But though she still retained the favour
of London audiences, her eighteen years' performances had probably not improved her voice ;
and when, in 1710, Handel formed a company for

the production of *Rinaldo*, Margarita was not one of the singers whom he thought fit to engage. Finding that she had lost favour, a great impresario of those days, Mr. Aaron Hill, treated her with but scant politeness. Margarita, like more than one prima donna of the present time, had a favourite parrot, and she taught the gifted bird to sing the first line of Handel's *Giulio Cesare :* "Non e vago." In rude allusion to the fact that the parrot was often seen at the open window of Mdlle. de l'Epine's house—whence he poured forth his melodious strains to the admiration of the passers by—Mr. Hill, having occasion to write to her, addressed his letter to "Mdlle. de l'Epine, at the sign of the Italian parrot." Enraged at this insult, she wrote back declining to have any further dealings with him, to which he replied that he could "very well spare her if she would send her feathered pupil."

In spite of this little incident, Margarita continued to sing, and in 1714 she appeared, doubtless to her own disadvantage, side by side with the rising star, Anastasia Robinson, in the opera of *Creso.* She went on singing, however, and it was not until 1722, when she had been thirty years on the stage, that the public was to hear the last of her.

Katherine Tofts and Margarita de l'Epine were succeeded, then, by Anastasia Robinson, who for some years was our leading singer in Italian opera. She was the daughter of a Mr. Robinson, a portrait-painter of merit who, having gone to Rome to study the pictorial art, acquired there a knowledge of music. He educated his two daughters with great care as singers. One of them married at an early age a Colonel Bowles, and retired from "the profession." The other, Anastasia, achieved great success and filled the principal parts in Italian opera from 1714 to 1724, when, being already secretly married to the distinguished commander, Lord Peterborough (who proved himself in Spain one of the most rapid marchers and most energetic fighters ever known), she abandoned the stage.

Her withdrawal is said to have been hurried by some ridiculous protestations of love, followed by unseemly familiarities, on the part of the male soprano, Senesino. Enraged at this ignoble rivalry, Lord Peterborough caned the offender behind the scenes till he fell on his knees and yelled for mercy. This strange affair is noticed by Lady Mary Wortley Montague in one of her letters. "The second heroine," she says, meaning Anastasia Robinson, "has engaged half the town in arms from the nicety of her virtue, which was not able to bear too near approach of Senesino in the opera, and her condescension in her acceptance of Lord Peterborough for a champion, who has signalized both his love and courage upon this occasion in as many instances as ever Don Quixote did for Dulcinea. Poor Senesino, like a vanquished giant, was forced to confess upon his knees that Anastasia was a non-pareil of virtue and beauty. Lord Stanhope (after-wards Lord Chesterfield), as dwarf to the said giant, joked on his side, and was challenged for his pains."

Though legally married to Anastasia, Lord Peterborough thought it beneath his dignity to acknowledge her as his wife. The fact that he was married to her seems, however, to have been an open secret; for the entertainments given by the Earl of Peterborough, over which Anastasia Robinson, as she was still called, presided, were attended by persons of the best repute. This eccentric nobleman had a passion for cooking, which he attributed to his having been frequently obliged, when he was in Spain, to prepare his own dinner.

"Such was the force of habit," says the ingenious Hawkins, "that till disabled by age his dinner was constantly of his own dressing. Those who have dined with him at Parson's Green say that he had a dress for that purpose, like that of a tavern cook, and that he used to retire from his company an hour before dinner time, and, having despatched his culinary affairs, would return properly dressed and take his place among them."

At last, in 1735, Lord Peterborough fell danger-ously ill, and being at Mount Bevis, near Southampton, begged his wife to come to him. She would only do so on condition that, while still keeping to her maiden name, she might at least be allowed to wear her wedding ring. This, after a struggle, he consented to. Then he was advised by his physicians to go to Lisbon, and here Anastasia refused absolutely to accompany him unless he recognized her publicly as his wife. Without telling her of his resolution, he begged her to meet a party of his relatives and friends at St. James's Palace, in an apartment occupied by one of his nephews, Mr. Pointz. When the company had assembled, the Earl rose and made a speech in honour of " Miss Anastasia Robinson." He rendered the fullest justice to her many excellent qualities, and ended by declaring that he had at length determined to do what he ought to have done long before : to declare his marriage, and present her to all his friends as his wife. With such energy and such feeling did he speak, that poor Anastasia, quite unprepared for the scene, fainted away.

Lord and Lady Peterborough went to Lisbon ; but the Earl did not long survive the voyage. After his death Anastasia retired to Mount Bevis, where, with the exception of a few visits to her early friend, the Duchess of Portsmouth, she passed the rest of her life. Her husband's memoirs came into her hands ; but after looking through them she decided not to offer them to the public. They would scarcely have redounded to his credit, for they are said to have contained his confession that before attaining the age of twenty he had committed three capital crimes.

Lavinia Fenton ought not, perhaps, to be classed with prime donne. But she married an English Duke, and cannot, therefore, be treated as a person of doubtful merit. She was not the Adelina Patti, but rather the Florence St. John of her time ; very pretty, very captivating, and quite as successful by her dramatic as by her musical talent. She sang at a very early age, and before she had learned to read could warble with charming expression all the popular airs of the day. Sent to school until the age of thirteen, she returned home to study music and singing. She had a passion for the stage, and at the age of eighteen came out at the Haymarket as "Monimia," in the *Orphan.* A permanent salary was at once offered to her, and such was the effect of her beauty and grace that propositions of everything except marriage were made to her from the most distinguished quarters. Soon after her first appearance she made a striking success in the attractive part of " Cherry " in Farquhar's *Beaux' Stratagem.* An engagement at increased terms was now pressed upon her by Rich, the manager of a rival theatre ; and the extravagantly liberal offer of fifteen shillings a week was found so tempting as to be irresistible.

Lavinia had only been a couple of years on the stage when, in 1728, the *Beggar's Opera* was put into rehearsal, the principal female part being assigned to the rising actress and singer of the day. It had occurred to Swift what an "odd pretty sort of a thing" a Newgate pastoral would make. Gay, to whom these words were addressed, thought the matter over, and decided, by no means to Swift's satisfaction, to carry out the idea in the form, not of a pastoral, but of a comedy with songs. Pope seems to have been of the same opinion as Swift. But they were both greatly interested in the welfare of their light-minded friend (whom Providence, as Swift put it, "had never intended to be more than two-and-twenty"); and as he seemed determined to go on with the work they occasionally gave him advice, and even wrote for him a few songs. "When you censure the age" has been attributed to Swift. "As the modes of the Court" passed for the work of Lord Chesterfield, and Sir Charles Williams was said to have written "Virgins are like the flower."

Gay offered the *Beggar's Opera* in the first instance to Congreve, the lessee of Drury Lane, who declined to bring it out. He was of opinion that it would "either take greatly or be damned confoundedly," and seems to have thought the chances about equal. The part of "Captain Macheath"—to be associated at a later period with tenors of the first rank like Sims Reeves—was originally undertaken

by the comedian Quin, who, though he was equal to
a convivial song, had no claim to be considered a
vocalist. After a few rehearsals, however, Quin
resigned the post in favour of a Mr. Robert Walker,
who possessed a good voice, and sang "Macheath's"
songs with so much success that he became the
roaring lion of supper parties, and was so much
made of that within a comparatively short space of
time he died of drink.

It was "Polly," however, as impersonated by the
fascinating Lavinia Fenton, that made the success
of the piece. She dressed the part in the most
simple manner ; and the pathetic *naïveté* with
which she delivered the lines —

> For on the rope that hangs my dear
> Depends poor Polly's life

had such an effect that applause burst forth from
every part of the house. The work had up to this
moment gone but poorly. Its triumph was now
assured, and the enthusiasm of the public went on
increasing until the fall of the curtain. The opera
soon made its way to Wales, Scotland, and Ireland.
The principal songs were inscribed on fans and
screens, and the enemies of foreign art boasted
that the *Beggar's Opera* (which is really a semi-
burlesque comedy interspersed with songs set to
popular tunes) had driven out the opera of the
Italians. The crowded houses drawn by Gay's
work must have had some effect in diminishing the

attendance of other theatres; and Arbuthnot, who appreciated dramatic music, says distinctly, in a paper on the subject, that the English had no taste for opera, properly so called, and that all they really cared for was their own national music in the form of popular songs. Nevertheless, it seems tolerably certain that Italian opera would have collapsed at the King's Theatre in the year 1728 whether or not the *Beggar's Opera* had been brought out. The sum of £50,000, subscribed six or seven years before to enable Handel to carry on the Italian opera at that time directed by him, had just been exhausted ; and without fresh funds the enterprise, even if the *Beggar's Opera* had never been heard of, could not have been kept going.

The *Beggar's Opera* was, in any case, triumphant, and the success of Lavinia Fenton went beyond that of the work itself. She was made the subject of numerous and in some cases highly fantastic biographies; collections were made of witticisms which she had never uttered ; she was the favourite toast at every convivial gathering; and such was the enthusiasm with which she inspired the gilded youth of the period that devoted admirers agreed to form themselves into a body-guard to see her safely home from the theatre. Under these circumstances Rich could not but show himself munificent. He raised the salary of his inimitable "Polly" to thirty shillings.

In spite of the body-guard, in spite even of thirty shillings a week, the Duke of Bolton succeeded in carrying off the adored one. Her singing in the air " O ponder well" had so enchanted him that he declared himself unable to live without her; and in obedience to this, or perhaps some better reason, Lavinia left the theatre and became as nearly a duchess as was possible in connection with a Duke already married. Swift tells the story of the elopement in his own matter-of-fact way :—" The Duke of Bolton," he writes, " has run away with ' Polly Peachum,' having settled £400 a year on her during pleasure, and upon disagreement £200 more."

Lavinia Fenton, putting aside the irremediable fault of her position, seems to have behaved as well as, under the circumstances, was possible. In a note to one of Swift's letters a favourable account of her is given by Mr. Joseph Wharton.

" She was," he says, " a very accomplished and most agreeable companion, had much wit, good strong sense, and just taste in polite literature. I have had the pleasure of being at table with her when her conversation was much admired by the first characters of the day, particularly by Lord Bathurst and Lord Grenville."

A story is told of a highly dramatic quarrel between Miss Fenton and the Duke, which was brought to a happy termination by Lavinia's own ingenuity. She remembered that it was as "Polly Peachum" that she had first attracted his attention. She dressed herself, when she was about to leave him, in the costume which had so fascinated him some years before, and sang, in her most pathetic manner, " O, what pain it is to part." Her tender accents, together with the recollections they awakened, were too much for his Grace. He was completely overcome, and, folding " Polly Peachum " in his arms, begged her never more to think of deserting him. Independently of its emotional effect, this ingeniously got-up scene must, if the Duke possessed any sense of humour, have greatly amused him. But he was seriously attached to Miss Fenton, and after the Duchess's death married her. The new Duchess survived her elevation to the position of wife nine years.

Gay's profits from the *Beggar's Opera*, though far from insignificant, were little enough compared with what an author of high reputation gains in the present day by a good play, well acted and sold under advantageous conditions. Some particulars on this subject may not be without interest.

On 15th February, 1727-8, Gay wrote to Swift : " I have deferred writing to you from time to time till I could give an account of the *Beggar's Opera.* It is acted at the playhouse in Lincoln's Inn Fields with such success that the playhouse has been crowded every night. To-night is the fifteenth time of acting, and it is thought that it will run a fortnight longer. I have ordered Motte [Benjamin Motte, the bookseller] to send the play to you the first opportunity. I make no interest, neither for approbation or money, nor has anybody been pressed to take tickets for my benefit; notwithstanding which I think I shall make an addition to my fortune of between six and seven hundred pounds. I know this account will give you pleasure, as I have pushed through this precarious affair without servility or flattery. . . . Lord Cobham says that I should have printed it in Italian over against the English, that the ladies might have understood what they read. The outlandish (as they call it) opera has been so thin of late that some have called that the *Beggar's Opera;* and if the run continues I fear I shall have remonstrances drawn up against me by the Royal Academy of Music."

"The *Beggar's Opera*," he wrote again, March 20th, 1727-8, " has been acted now thirty-six times, as was as full the last night as the first; and as yet there is not the least probability of a thin audience, though there is a discourse about the town that the directors of the Royal Academy of Music design to solicit against its being played on the outlandish opera days, as it is now called. On the benefit day of one of the actors last week, one of the players falling sick, they were obliged to give out another play or dismiss the audience. A play was given out, but the audience called out for the

Beggar's Opera, and they were forced to play it or the audience would not have stayed.

" I have got by this success between seven and eight hundred pounds; and Rich (deducting the whole charge of the house) has acquired already near four thousand pounds. In about a month I am going to the Bath with the Duchess of Marlborough and Mr. Congreve, for I have no expectations of receiving any favours from the Court. The Duchess of Queensberry is in Wiltshire, where she has had the small-pox in so favourable a way that she has not above seven or eight on her face; she is now perfectly recovered. There is a mezzotinto print published to-day of ' Polly,' the heroine of the *Beggar's Opera,* who was before unknown, and now in so high vogue, that I am in doubt whether her fame does not surpass that of the opera itself. I would not have talked so much upon this subject or upon anything that regards myself but to you; but as I know you interest yourself so sincerely in everything that concerns me, I believe you would have blamed me if I had said less."

When, the run of the piece still continuing, Gay had received a clear thousand pounds, Swift, Pope, Arbuthnot, and other friends of his seemed to think that he had already amassed a fortune; and they held a consultation with him as to what should be done with it. Mr. Lewis advised him to place it in the funds and live upon the interest; Pope recom-

mended the purchase of an annuity; while Dr. Arbuthnot, who knew to which course Gay was by nature
most inclined, told him " to live upon the principal
and trust to Providence." Meanwhile the success
of the opera continued. " It has been acted," wrote
Pope, on the 23rd of March, 1727-8, "near forty
days running, and will certainly continue the whole
season. So he has more than a fence about his
thousand pounds. He will soon be thinking of a
fence about his two thousand."

Swift was strongly in favour of an annuity. In
a letter to Gay, dated " Dublin, November 27th,
1727," he in the first place speaks of the *Beggar's
Opera :* " I did not understand," he says, " that the
sum of Lockit and Peachum's quarrel was an
imitation of the one between Brutus and Cassius till
I was told of it. I wish Macheath, when he was
going to be hanged, had imitated Alexander the
Great when he was dying. I would have had his
fellow rogues desire his commands about a successor,
and him to answer : 'Let it be the most worthy,' &c.
We have a million stories about the opera, of the
applause of the song 'that was levelled at me,'
when two first ministers were in a box together
and all the world staring at them." The utterer of
this remark was, it need scarcely be said, Sir Robert
Walpole.

Then, turning to the subject of Gay's private
affairs, Swift adds : "I am glad your opera hath

mended your purse, though it may spoil your court. With your desire, my Lord Bolingbroke, Mr. Pulteney, and Mr. Pope do command you to buy an annuity with two thousand pounds that you may laugh at courts and first ministers. Ever preserve some spice of the Alderman, and prepare against age and dulness, and sickness, or illness, or death of friends. . . . An old decayed poet is a creature obedient and at mercy where he can find none."

For a time Gay seems to have followed the pleasant advice of Dr. Arbuthnot. "Mr. Gay's fame continues," wrote Mrs. Martha Blount on the 7th of May, 1727-8, to Swift, "but his riches are in a fair way of diminishing; he has gone to the Bath." To "the Bath" Gay was followed by his work. "The *Beggar's Opera*," he wrote to Swift, "is acted here, but our 'Polly' has got no fame, though the actors have got money. I have sent by Dr. Delaney the opera, 'Polly Peachum,' and 'Captain Macheath.' I would have sent you my own head (which is now engraved to make up the gang) but it is not yet finished. I suppose you must have heard that I have had the honour to have had a sermon preached against my works by a Court chaplain, which I look upon as no small addition to my fame." The chaplain here referred to was Dr. Thomas Herring, then preacher to the society in Lincoln's Inn, and afterwards Archbishop of Canterbury. Swift, in the third number of the *Intelligencer*, scourges Dr.

Herring in his severest style on account of his sermon against the *Beggar's Opera.*

" I am assured," wrote Swift, " that several clergymen in this city went privately to see the *Beggar's Opera* represented ; and that the fleering coxcombs in the pit amused themselves with making discoveries and spreading the names of those gentlemen round the audience. I shall not pretend to vindicate a clergyman who would appear openly in his habit at a theatre with such a vicious crew as might probably stand round him at such comedies and profane tragedies as are often represented. Besides, I know very well that persons of their function are bound to avoid the appearance of evil, or of giving cause of offence. But when the Lords Chancellors, who are keepers of the king's conscience; when the judges of the land, whose title is reverend ; when ladies, who are bound by the rules of their sex to the strictest decency, appear in the theatre without censure; I cannot understand why a young clergyman who comes concealed out of curiosity to see an innocent and moral play should be so highly condemned; nor do I much approve of the rigour of a great prelate who said ' he hoped none of his clergy were there.' I am glad to hear there are no weightier objections against the reverend body planted in this city, and I hope there never may. But I should be very sorry that any of them should be so weak as to imitate a Court

chaplain in England who preached against the
Beggar's Opera, which will probably do more good
than a thousand sermons of so stupid, so injudicious,
and so prostitute a divine."

He concluded in the true spirit of a friend :
" Upon the whole, I deliver my judgment, that
nothing but servile attachment to a party, affectation of singularity, lamentable dulness, mistaken
zeal, or studied hypocrisy can have the least reasonable objection against this excellent moral performance of the celebrated Mr. Gay."

" I suppose," writes Swift to Pope, in reference
to Gay's sojourn at Bath, " I suppose Mr. Gay will
return from the Bath with twenty pounds more flesh
and two hundred less in money. Providence never
designed him to be above two-and-twenty by his
thoughtlessness and cullibility. He has as little
foresight of age, sickness, poverty, or loss of
admirers as a girl of fifteen."

In spite of Gay's notorious carelessness on the
subject of money, Swift entrusted him with considerable sums for investments, which seem to
have taken the form of loans to great personages.
" Your money," wrote Gay to Swift, " with part of
my own, is still in the hands of Lord Bathurst,
which I believe he will keep no longer, but repay it
on his coming to town, when I will endeavour to
dispose of it as I do of my own unless I receive your
orders to the contrary." Gay's usual method of

" disposing " of his own money was spending it. "I will leave my money," answered Swift, "in Lord Bathurst's hands, and the management of it (for want of better) in yours; and pray keep the interest money in a bag wrapped up by itself for fear of your own fingers under your carelessness. I hope," continued Swift, " when you are rich enough, you will have some little economy of your own in town and country, and be able to give your friends a pint of port; for the domestic season of life will come on. I wish you had a little villakin in this neighbourhood; but you are yet too volatile, and any lady with a coach and six horses would carry you to Japan."

Gay, meanwhile, had been staying with the Duchess of Marlborough, at Bath. " I have had a very severe attack of fever," he writes, December 2nd, 1728, " which, by the care of our friend, Dr. Arbuthnot, has, I hope, almost left me. I have been confined about ten days, but never to my bed, so that I hope soon to get abroad about my business, that is the care of the second part of the *Beggar's Opera*, which was almost ready for rehearsal; but which received the Duke of Grafton's commands (upon the information that he was rehearsing a play unproper to be represented) not to rehearse any new play whatever until his Grace had seen it. What will become of it I know not, but I am sure I have written nothing that can be legally suppressed unless the setting vices in general in an odious light and virtue in an amiable one may give offence. I passed five or six months this year at the Bath with the Duchess of Marlborough, and then, in the view of taking care of myself, wrote this piece. If it goes on, in case of success, I have taken care to make better terms for myself. I tell you this, because I know you are so good as to interest yourself so warmly in my affairs, that it is what you want to know."

"I had never much opinion of your vamped play," wrote Swift, in reply, "although Mr. Pope seemed to have, and although it were ever so good. But you should have done like the parson and changed your text, I mean your title and the names of the persons. After all it was the effect of idleness, for you are in the prime of life when invention and judgment go together."

Stimulated, and at the same time held in check by the exhortations and the gibes of his friends, Gay succeeded in keeping together what for him was a considerable sum of money. In 1729 he wrote to Swift informing him that he had now three thousand pounds in his possession. " Mr. Gay assures me," says Swift in a letter to Pope, " his £3,000 is kept entire and sacred." Gay had now changed his ducal associates. "He has been all this summer," writes Swift, "with the Duke and Duchess of Queensberry. He is the same man, so is every one here that you know : mankind is unamendable."

Contrary to the expectations of his literary friends, Gay, who notwithstanding his levity of character had probably not forgotten his losses some years before in the South Sea bubble, neither risked nor squandered the money he had made by the *Beggar's Opera* and by *Polly*, its unacted sequel, which, though its representation was forbidden, was sold largely in printed form to private subscribers.

The Duchess of Queensberry made much of him; and he continued to enjoy her society and to live in her house until, in 1732—four or five years after the production of the *Beggar's Opera*—he died. Meanwhile he had falsified the predictions of Swift, had abstained from following the ironical advice of Arbuthnot, and had even gone beyond the prudent counsel of Pope. He neither bought an annuity, nor "lived on the principal"—nor even on the interest. He saved his money and lived on his friends.

He remembered, too, let us hope, that he owed a good part of his fortune to the talent and grace of Lavinia Fenton, the first impersonator of "Polly."

CHAPTER III.

CUZZONI AND FAUSTINA.

THE seasons 1723 and 1724 were important ones
in the history of our Italian opera. Durastanti,
after a series of brilliant successes, withdrew before
the superior attractions of the newly-arrived Cuzzoni; and the advent of this famous vocalist seems
also to have corresponded with the retirement
of Anastasia Robinson. Durastanti had enjoyed
great popularity among the aristocratic patrons
of the opera, and it is recorded in the *Evening
Post* of March 7, 1721, that "last Thursday, His
Majesty was pleased to stand godfather, and the
Princess and the Lady Bruce godmothers, to a
daughter of Mrs. Durastanti, chief singer in the
opera house : the Marquis Visconti for the king,
and Lady Lichfield for the Princess." The chief
patron of " Mrs." Durastanti (the English had not
at that time acquired the absurd habit of calling

foreign gentlemen Monsieur, Signor, or Herr,* nor of giving the title of Madame even to English-women) was that same Earl of Peterborough who, a year after Durastanti's departure from England, married Anastasia Robinson; and on the occasion of her farewell performance he requested Pope to write for her a parting address, which she recited from the stage, and which ended with these lines :—

> But let old charmers yield to new;
> Happy soil, adieu, adieu.

Cuzzoni had been specially engaged by Handel; and she made her first appearance in *Ottone,* one of his most successful operas. She was received with such enthusiasm that the directors, who had engaged to pay her two thousand guineas for the season, thought themselves justified in raising the prices for the second performance to four guineas a ticket. Delighted with her talent, Handel composed a number of airs to suit the peculiarities of her voice and style. She, on the other hand, treated the composer with but scanty respect; making alterations in the passages he had written, and affecting inability to sing them in their original form. At last, on one famous occasion, the composer lost all patience with her, and, seizing her by the waist, threatened, unless she would sing what had been set down for her, to

---

* The folly of this custom becomes apparent when for general convenience it is found necessary to designate by the equivalent of " Mr." a Russian, a Hungarian, or a Pole.

throw her out of window. This display of energy
and decision had the effect of bringing the capricious
prima donna to her senses. One of the airs which
Handel wrote for this ungrateful woman (" Affanni
del pensier," in *Ottone*) was so beautiful that, according to an eminent musician—Mainwaring, who was
not at the time on good terms with Handel—the
" great bear was certainly inspired when he wrote
that song."

Cuzzoni had neither face nor figure to recom-
mend her. But such was the effect of her singing
that the subscribers to the opera were enchanted
with her, and showed themselves ready to obey her
whims and fancies, even in the smallest particulars.
She has been accused by the author of an *essai sur
la musique*, of " turbulent and obstinate temper,"
of " ingratitude and insolence." The writer declares
that she once begged an English gentleman to give
her a suit of lace ; but " not liking it when sent to
her," had the audacity to throw it into the fire.

Handel, besides being a sublime composer, was
an excellent manager and a thorough man of business. He possessed enough knowledge of human
nature, moreover, to understand instinctively how
a prima donna who gave herself airs should be
treated. Cuzzoni was without a rival, Handel
determined to find her one, and he did not rest
until he had engaged a singer whose successes in
Italy warranted him in the belief that she would

not only attain the same popularity as Cuzzoni, but probably eclipse her.

Faustina Bordoni, a vocalist who was to render Handel the greatest services, both of a direct and indirect kind, was a Venetian lady of noble birth, a pupil of Marcello and Gasparini. She was beautiful, graceful, had charming manners, and though she had been some years on the stage was not more than twenty-six when she made her first appearance in London. During the season of 1725 such had been the rage for Cuzzoni, especially in *Rodelinda*, that every lady in the fashionable world adopted the brown silk dress embroidered with silver which she wore as the heroine of that opera. "For a year," says Dr. Burney, "the dress seemed a national uniform of youth and beauty."

Cuzzoni appears at this time to have commanded almost as high terms as would be offered to a prima donna in the present day, for she is said to have refused a salary of 240,000 livres (francs) for one season from a manager in Italy. When, however, in 1726, Faustina appeared, the dominion of Cuzzoni was shaken. It has been said that the new comer possessed charms of person and manner in which Cuzzoni seems to have been altogether wanting, though it is difficult to believe that she did not at times depart from her unconciliatory demeanour. Dr. Burney describes Cuzzoni's voice as "clear, sweet, and flexible," adding that it was difficult to say whether she most excelled in slow or in rapid parts. " A native warble enabled her to execute divisions with such facility as to conceal every appearance of difficulty, and so soft and touching was the natural tone of her voice that she rendered pathetic whatever she sang, in which she had leisure to unfold the whole volume. The art of conducting, sustaining, increasing, and diminishing her tones by minute degrees acquired for her among professors the title of complete mistress of her art. In a cantabile air, though the notes she added were few, she never lost a favourable opportunity of enriching the cantilena with all the refinements and embellishments of the time. Her shake was perfect, she had a creative fancy, and the power of occasionally accelerating and retarding the measure in the most artificial manner by what the Italians call *tempo rubato.* Her high notes were unrivalled in clearness and sweetness, and her intonations were so just and fixed that it seemed as if it were not in her power to sing out of tune."

" Faustina," says the doctor, reproducing what the flute-player Quantz (historically known as teacher of the flute to Frederick the Great) had told him, " possessed a mezzo-soprano that was less clear than penetrating. Her compass now was only from B flat to G in alt, but after this time she extended its limits downwards. Her execution was articulate and brilliant. She had a fluent tongue for pronouncing words rapidly and distinctly, and a flexible throat for divisions, with so beautiful a shake that she put it in motion upon short notice, just when she would. The passages might be smooth, or by leaps, or consisting of iterations of the same note, their execution was equally easy to her as to any instrument whatever. She was, doubtless, the first who introduced with success a repetition of the same note. She sang adagios with great passion and expression, but was not equally successful if such deep sorrow were to be impressed on the hearers as might require dragging, sliding, or notes of syncopation, and *tempo rubato.* She had a very happy memory in arbitrary changes and embellishments, and a clear and quick judgment in giving to words their full power and expression. In her action she was very happy, and, as her performance possessed that flexibility of muscles and features which constitutes face-play, she succeeded equally well in furious, amorous, and tender parts. In short, she was born for singing and acting."

Faustina enjoyed the advantage of having Handel on her side, and she had the good sense and good taste not to reject, as her rival had done, the airs which the great master composed expressly for her. The musical public seized with joy the opportunity of splitting up into two parties. As Margarita de l'Epine and Katherine Tofts had before been worshipped by separate bands of devoted partisans, so Cuzzoni and

Faustina were now adored by rival bodies of sworn
devotees. The Cuzzoni party was led by the
Countess of Pembroke; the supporters of Faustina
were headed by the Countess of Burlington and
Lady Delawar. The beautiful Faustina had the
men on her side. Cuzzoni was taken up by the
women. On one occasion (mentioned by Horace
Walpole), at a party to which both Cuzzoni and
Faustina had been invited, it was impossible to settle
the question of precedence between them. At a
later date, when a like difference of opinion was
raised as to which of four eminent dancers should
be considered the first, Mr. Lumley, manager of
Her Majesty's Theatre, made the insidious and
perfectly effective suggestion that it was for the
youngest to give way. This idea does not seem to
have been thought of in connection with Faustina
and Cuzzoni. Neither would sing in presence of
the other; and it was found necessary to make
Cuzzoni believe that Faustina had left the house,
Faustina being afterwards persuaded that Cuzzoni
had done the same, before either of them would
consent to appear.

The Cuzzoni-Faustina rivalry had in one instance the effect of separating husband and wife,
for Sir Robert Walpole having espoused the
cause of Faustina, his wife felt bound to support
Cuzzoni. Lady Walpole, in the absence of her
husband, asked both of them to dinner; and the

chroniclers of the period relate, with expressions of astonishment, that the rival songstresses got through the evening without quarrelling. At last, however, meeting face to face on the stage in a performance designed specially to exhibit them in this close companionship, the applause and counter-applause from the public so excited them that they fell upon one another and could not be separated until each had suffered some personal damage at the hands of her antagonist. In a struggle of this kind the beautiful Faustina must, of course, have suffered more than the plain Cuzzoni.

The appearance of Faustina seems to have been the signal for the riot, which was commemorated in the following epigram :—

> Old poets sing that beasts did dance
> Whenever Orpheus played ;
> So to Faustina's charming voice
> Wise Pembroke's asses brayed.

The encounter was made the subject of a farce called *The Contretemps*, in which the prime donne were represented as contending queens. Faustina ends by chasing Cuzzoni from the stage, while Handel looks on unconcerned, like the backwoodsman's wife, who seeing her husband engaged with a bear, declared that she " did not care which whipped."

The rivalry having now degenerated into direct personal hostility, the directors of the Opera thought it time to separate the two enemies, and it was resolved, as one of them must leave the country, to get rid of the least attractive. Cuzzoni was so considered. She had solemnly sworn never to accept a smaller salary than Faustina, and they had hitherto been equally paid. The directors now offered an extra guinea to Faustina, and Cuzzoni, whether from wounded vanity or respect for her plighted word, retired from the theatre. On the occasion of her departure from England the following lines were addressed to her by Ambrose Phillips :—

> Little siren of the stage,
> Charmer of an idle age,
> Empty warbler, breathing lyre,
> Wanton gale of fond desire,
> Bane of every manly art,
> Sweet enfeebler of the heart,
> O, too pleasing is thy strain ;
> Hence to southern climes again !
> Tuneful mischief, vocal spell,
> To this island bid farewell ;
> Leave us as we ought to be,
> Leave the Britons rough and free.

Leaving the Britons " rough and free," Cuzzoni undertook in 1728 a series of tours on the Continent, but came back to re-enslave her London admirers in 1734, when she sang at the opera-house in Lincoln's Inn Fields established by Porpora in opposition to Handel. Then she again went abroad. Returning, however, to England a third time, in 1750, she met with but little success.

She had lost her voice, and it has been asserted that "not even the enemies of Faustina would come to applaud her."

Cuzzoni was not one of the fortunate prime donne. She was not, indeed, destined for a tragic end like Sontag and Madame de Saint-Huberti; but her fate was in its way quite as sad. She had committed the mistake of marrying a harpsi-chord-maker named Sandoni; which, though her husband possessed some musical taste and even musical talent, was, for so great a singer, a *mésalliance*. It was reported at one time, in 1741, when she was singing on the Continent, that she had poisoned him, and was to be beheaded in consequence. But either the accusation was not proved or an acquittal was pronounced on the ground of justifiable homicide. Cuzzoni was, in any case, not executed, and when, eight years afterwards, she made her last appearance in England, no one seems to have paid any attention to the unpleasant rumour to which publicity had been given in the London *Daily Post* of September 7th, 1741.

Sandoni had now, in any case, disappeared. His wife's biographers make no further mention of him, nor is there much more to be recorded of Cuzzoni herself. She left England with the proceeds of her benefit—which seems to have been regarded less as a musical entertainment than as a work of charity —and went to Holland, where, having imprudently paid her debts with the money she had received in England, she fell once more into poverty and was thrown into gaol. The prison authorities, however, did the best they could for her under the circumstances. They allowed her to go out every night to sing at the theatre, and with the money thus earned she was eventually able to procure her liberation. At last the poor woman lost what little voice she had in the midst of her troubles still retained, and she was absolutely unable to sing. After maintaining herself for some time at Bologna by button-making, she died in obscurity. Her fate was apparently that of the stage-queens spoken of by the critic who, to Candide's question as to how such dignified persons were treated in France, replied : " On les adore quand elles sont belles, et on les jette a la voirie quand elles sont mortes."

The career of Faustina, on the other hand, can scarcely be said to have belied her auspicious name. No courtly honours were reserved for her ; but she became the wife of Hasse, a very distinguished composer, who, being appointed by Augustus King of Poland and Elector of Saxony, to direct the Dresden Opera-house, gave his wife a fifteen years' engagement at what was then the most famous lyrical theatre in Europe.

CHAPTER IV.

MINGOTTI AND GABRIELLI.

FAUSTINA, who had driven away Cuzzoni, who had expelled Durastanti, was, in accordance with the mutability of things and the evanescent nature of a prima donna's attractions, herself to disappear before a newer star. This was Caterina Mingotti, a pupil of Porpora, who for that and other reasons was hated by Hasse, the instructor, business agent, and husband of Faustina.

Regina Mingotti, born Valentini, was in her youth a servant-pupil at a convent. But she hated drudgery, and to escape housework resolved to turn to what account she could her fresh and beautiful voice. She began her career, as several prime donne have imprudently done, by marrying a manager; others having in like manner sacrificed themselves to the relentless enterprise of a singing master. Such marriages are, probably, to be explained less by pure folly on the part of the young vocalist than by a desire to be placed as soon and as advantageously as possible before the public. It was on an aged impresario named Mingotti that Regina Valentini threw herself away. Nor, strangely enough, does she appear to have done so with any view of appearing on the stage, her primary motive in getting married being simply to escape the labours imposed on her at the convent. But having once secured his prize, Mingotti placed the young girl under the tuition of Porpora, known as the rival at one time of Hasse, at another of Handel.

Mingotti's talent had, of course, no charm for Hasse; and in imitation of the professor in the Bourgeois Gentilhomme, who, wishing to revenge himself upon his rival, threatened that he would "tear him in the style of Juvenal"—*Je le déchirerai en style de Juvénal*—Hasse wrote a series of epigrams against Porpora, in one of which he declared, without any apparent point, that Mingotti was the last branch he had to cling to. Much cleverer than his epigrams against Hasse was a device of Porpora which he employed with the view of exhibiting the supposed weakness of Mingotti's voice. She was to appear in a new opera of Hasse's, and the treacherous maestro wrote for her an adagio which rose and fell upon the very notes which he considered the most doubtful in her really perfect voice. What, however, had been intended as a trap, served only to display Mingotti's exceptional merits both of voice and style.

When Mingotti appeared in London, her singing was such that, in the words of Burney, "it discovered her to be a perfect mistress of her art." Some, however, were of opinion that (again to quote Burney) she "would have been even more irresistible if she had had a little more female grace and softness."

Mingotti had made her first appearance at Dresden, and with so much success that Faustina's hurried retreat from that highly musical capital was attributed, probably not without reason, to jealousy. She was heard for the first time in London during the winter season of 1754; and her singing had the effect of reviving the fortunes of Italian opera in England, not, just before Mingotti's advent, very flourishing. Her husband had, apparently, departed from the theatre of this world. The manager of the London Opera-house was, at this time, Vaneschi, and a dispute between the impresario and the favourite vocalist gradually developed until at length it took the form of one of those feuds so frequent in the history of music.

The differences between Mingotti and her manager were terminated by the bankruptcy of the latter. Then this adventurous prima donna herself undertook the direction of the Opera-house, and, encountering the fate which has hitherto attended, with scarcely one exception, every operatic manager in England, lost all that she had invested in the enterprise. Happily she was not reduced, like poor Cuzzoni, to the necessity of doing manual labour for a livelihood. Dr. Burney, who called upon her in 1772 at Munich, where she had established herself, found that for an impoverished person she was occupying a very agreeable position. "She seemed," he says, "to live very comfortably, was well received at Court, and esteemed by all who were able to judge of her understanding and enjoy her conversation. It gave me great pleasure to hear her speak concerning practical music, which she does with so much intelligence as any *maestro di cappella* with whom I ever conversed. Her knowledge of singing and powers of expression in different styles are truly amazing, and must delight all such as can receive satisfaction from song, unconnected with the blandishments of youth and beauty. She speaks three languages—German, French, and Italian—so well that it is difficult to say which of them is her own. English she likewise speaks, and Spanish well enough to converse in them, and understands Latin, but in the three languages first mentioned she is truly eloquent."

Caterina Gabrielli, the last of the great prime donne who figured at our Italian Opera-house during the eighteenth century, was, sad to relate, the daughter of a cook. She was born at Rome. Her father was in the service of Gabrielli, the celebrated Cardinal, and it was through the good offices of his Eminence that the young girl was enabled to receive a musical education. Her father knew that Caterina possessed talent; but he was not rich enough to place her under a singing-master. He took her from time to time to the Argentina Theatre, where she heard good singers in the best operas; and such was her memory that on her return home she would repeat in her own untutored way the principal airs from these works. One day the Cardinal, walking in his garden, overheard her performances and was struck by them. The youthful Caterina was trilling forth an aria of Galuppi's, and with such brilliancy that the Cardinal made her go through her entire repertory, after which he determined to give her the best instruction that could be obtained.

He entrusted her, first to Garcia—Spagnoletto, as he was called—and afterwards to Porpora. Then, to complete her training, he sent her to the Conservatorio of Venice, the direction of which had recently passed from the hands of Galuppi to those of Sacchini.

At the age of seventeen she was considered fully equipped for appearing before the public, and she accepted an engagement at the Theatre of Lucca, where she sang with the greatest possible success the prima donna part in Galuppi's *Sofonisba*. She at once became, under the name of La Cuochetina, the favourite of the public. Not that there was

anything that savoured of the kitchen in her
demeanour. " There was such grace and dignity
in her gestures and deportment," writes Burney,
" as caught every unprejudiced eye ; indeed, she
filled the stage and occupied the attention of the
spectators so much that they could look at nothing
while she was in view." Her voice was of great
compass and is said to have been of perfect quality
throughout. She seems to have been what in the
present day would be called a light soprano ;
excelling in rapid, brilliant pieces, without being
equally successful in passages of expression. The
young noblemen of the Duchy of Lucca overwhelmed
her with attention, but she preferred to their society
that of her comrades in art.

She was invited to sing, one after the other, at
all the principal Opera-houses of Italy ; and, in 1750,
she appeared at the San Carlo of Naples, in the
Didone of Jomelli. Metastasio heard her and proposed to give her some lessons in the art of de-
claiming recitative. As he taught his charming
pupil he became more and more interested in her.
But the famous operatic poet was now fifty-three
years of age, and tormented by various maladies;
and in spite of his reputation as an agreeable man,
cherished by the powerful and adored by the
beautiful in all the Courts of Europe, he was unable
to make an impression on the young " cook girl."
At Metastasio's recommendation she was invited to

Vienna, and appointed Court-singer to the Emperor Francis. Here, as in the various Italian cities where she had sung, she found herself surrounded by admirers from whom, while preserving more or less perfectly the independence of her heart, she accepted without scruple the richest gifts. At Vienna the ambassadors of France and Portugal were the chief competitors for her favours. The Frenchman appears to have considered that he had claims upon her fidelity, and, to satisfy himself whether or not he was deceived, concealed himself in her house, where, to his indignation, he saw the Portuguese come from her apartment. Instead of killing his rival—which, if blood was to be shed, was evidently the proper thing to do—he attacked Gabrielli herself, and would have run her through the body with his sword but that the point of the weapon was stopped by the whalebone of her stays. In his onslaught, however, he had scratched her and at the sight of her blood he collapsed, falling upon his knees, and uttering volleys of imprecations on himself and of prayers to her. She consented to forgive him on condition of his presenting her with the sword with which he had wounded her, intending to preserve it as a trophy with the following inscription engraved upon it :—
" Epee de M—— qui osa frapper la Gabrielli."

A hundred years later, when Alphonse Karr was in like manner struck with a dagger by Madame

Louise Colet, a poetess whose verses he had failed
to admire, he took the poniard from her hand and
afterwards placed it above his mantelpiece, with
the inscription :—" Donné, dans le dos, par Madame
Louise Colet."

The French Ambassador, however, was to be
saved from the reproach prepared for him by
Gabrielli. He appealed to Metastasio, who inter-
vened and persuaded the offended singer to sur-
render the peccant weapon. Brydone, in his tour,
is thankful that Gabrielli's faults were apparent to
everyone who approached her, for otherwise, he
says, " she must have made dreadful havoc in the
world," though, " with all her deficiencies," he
adds, " she was supposed to have achieved more
conquests than any woman breathing."

At last she became so capricious that it was
difficult to make her sing at all, and almost impossible to make her sing her best. The recognized
expedient for bringing out her powers was to place
her favourite lover for the time being in a prominent
place either in the pit or in one of the boxes. Then,
if they were on good terms—which, however, was
seldom the case—she would address her tender
airs directly to him and would throw her whole soul
into the music. Some fatuous admirer of Gabrielli's
promised Brydone, when he was in Sicily, to show
him how perfectly this device acted. But Gabrielli,

suspecting, it is said, that he had boasted of his power, would take no notice of him.

The Viceroy of Sicily, wishing to show Gabrielli particular attention, invited her to dinner, and as she did not turn up at the proper time sent a special messenger to remind her that the hour had come. She was found lying on the sofa reading a book, and she declared that the engagement had entirely escaped her memory. The Viceroy was ready to overlook her rudeness; but in the evening, singing at the Opera-house, she showed herself intolerably capricious, acting negligently and singing all her airs in a whisper. The Viceroy sent word to her that he was seriously displeased, when she replied that he might force her to cry but could not compel her to sing. At last, exasperated by her obstinacy, he sent her to prison for twelve days. Here she entertained her fellow-captives, paid their debts, gave them money for themselves, and sang her finest songs in the finest style every day until, amid the rejoicings of the grateful prisoners, she was liberated.

A few years afterwards the capricious vocalist was again to be incarcerated. This was at Parma, where she was on the best terms with the Infante Don Ferdinand. He made her the most costly presents, and, though he was a hunchback, his munificence reconciled her to his want of personal

attractions. He, on the other hand, was tormented
by jealousy, and scarcely an hour of the day passed
without a quarrel between them. After one of
these disputes he locked her up in her room for
several days together. On another occasion, when
they had had a terrible scene about an English
nobleman whose rivalry displeased the prince,
Gabrielli called him an " accursed hunchback ; "
upon which the " gobbo maladetto " went out of
the room, slammed the door and locked it. Then
he ordered her to be carried to prison. But on
entering what she supposed to be the gaol she
found that the rooms were furnished with the
utmost magnificence, and that a number of servants
were in readiness to take her orders. The Infante
had improvised a prison in his own palace, and
Gabrielli had scarcely entered it when he waited
upon her, in the hope of making his peace. The
enraged singer, however, would have nothing to
say to him, and when he left her she got out of
a window into a garden, scaled the garden walls,
and made her escape.

Gabrielli now went to Russia, where Catherine II.
received her with the greatest warmth. When the
Empress began to discuss with the prima donna the
terms of her engagement and found that they were
excessive, she said in amazement: " Why, I do
not give so much to my Field Marshals." " Get
your Field Marshals to sing for you," replied

Gabrielli. Catherine took the retort in good part, and Gabrielli received the salary she had asked. She left Russia laden with presents; her pockets full of money, and her jewel-case full of diamonds.

She now visited England, but did not without some hesitation accept the invitation that had been sent her. " I should not be mistress of my own will," she said, " and whenever I might have a fancy not to sing the people would insult and perhaps molest me. It is better to remain unmolested, were it even in a prison." She was now forty-five years of age. She had been singing since the age of seventeen, and it possibly occurred to her that, appearing for the first time on a new stage in an unfamiliar country, she would not meet with success. The disposition not to sing did, as she had anticipated, assert itself. But the English do not seem either to have molested or insulted her. During her stay in London she appeared in Sacchini's *Didone*, Piccini's *Cajo Mario*, and Vento's *Vestale*. Lord Mount Edgcumbe, who heard her in *Didone*, was not much struck by her singing, while as to her acting, what he chiefly observed was that she took the greatest possible care of her enormous hoop as she sidled into the flames of Carthage. Brydone declares that it was not caprice alone that prevented her at times from singing. " That wonderful flexibility of voice," he adds, " that runs with such rapidity and neatness through the most minute divisions, and produces almost instantaneously so great a variety of modulation, must assuredly depend on the very nicest tones of the fibres ; and, if these are in the smallest degree relaxed or their elasticity diminished, how is it possible that their contractions and expansions can so readily obey the will as to produce these effects?"

Gabrielli made but a brief stay in London. She returned to Italy, where she continued to sing until the year 1780. Thus she remained on the stage until the somewhat advanced age of fifty. She survived her retirement sixteen years. Gabrielli had a sister named Francesca, whom she used to take about with her, and who replaced her on those occasions when she was unwilling or unable to sing. With all her caprices she had many good points : she gave largely in charity and took great care of her parents in their old age. She also paid the expenses of her brother's musical education; though the money so invested was not destined to yield good results. He on one occasion sang at the Argentina Theatre as a tenor. Scarcely had he begun his first air when the audience began to hiss and hoot; then cries were raised of "Away, you raven." The singer, however, was not to be put down by vulgar clamour. With the greatest calmness he advanced to the footlights and said :—
" You fancy you are mortifying me by hooting me;

you are greatly deceived; on the contrary, I applaud your judgment, for I solemnly declare to you that I never appear on any stage without receiving the same treatment, and sometimes much worse."

But I am not writing the history of the tenor.

CHAPTER V.

SOPHIE ARNOULD.

BESIDES being one of the wittiest and most charming of women, Sophie Arnould was the most distinguished of the vocalists who sang at the Paris Opera in the old days before France had become one of the three great musical countries of Europe. During the eighteenth century, at least until the arrival of Gluck in Paris, music, especially operatic music and oratorio, was, thanks to Handel, on a much higher level in England than in France. All the great Italian singers visited London and sang at the King's Theatre. France, on the other hand, was without an Italian Opera; and its National Opera, to judge from the accounts of it left by Rousseau and by Burney, was not a thing to be proud of. "The drama," says Halévy, the composer of *La Juive*, in his *Origines de l'Opéra en France*, "comprises but a small number of scenes, the pieces are of a briefness to be envied; it is music summarized; two

phrases make an air. The task of the composer
then was far from being what it is now. The
secret had not yet been discovered of those pieces,
those finales which have been so admirably developed, linking together in one well-conceived
whole a variety of situations which assist the
inspiration of the composer and sometimes call it
forth. There is certainly more music in one of the
finales of a modern work than in the five acts of an
opera of Lulli's. We may add that the art of
instrumentation, since carried to such a high
degree of brilliancy, was then confined within very
narrow limits ; or rather the art did not exist.
The violins, violas, bass viols, hautboys, which at
first formed the entire arsenal of the composer,
seldom did more than follow the voices. Lulli,
moreover, wrote only the vocal part and the bass of
his compositions. His pupils, Lalouette and Colasse,
who were conductors (*chefs d'orchestre*, or, as was
said at that time, *batteurs de mesure*) under his
orders, filled up the orchestral parts in accordance
with his indications. This explains how, in the
midst of all the details with which he had to occupy
himself, he could write such a great number of works;
but it does not diminish the idea one must form of
his facility, his intelligence, and his genius, for
these works, rapidly as they were composed, kept
possession of the stage for more than a century."
Lulli was succeeded at the French Opera by

Rameau, who, in the words of Halévy, "elevated and strengthened the art. His harmonies were more solidly woven; his orchestra was richer; his instrumentation more skilful; his colouring more decided."

Dr. Burney, however, who visited Paris at a time when Rameau's works were constantly being performed, speaks of the music he heard at the Paris Opera as monotonous in the extreme and without rhythm or expression. The French journals of the middle of the eighteenth century loved to assure their readers that Rameau was the first musician in Europe, though, as Grimm remarked, "Europe scarcely knew the name of her first musician, knew none of his operas, and could not have tolerated them." As for Dr. Burney, he found nothing at the French Opera to admire but the dancing and the decorations, "and these alone," he says, "seemed to give pleasure to the audience."

In Italy during the eighteenth century the prima donna was a personage of almost as much importance as everywhere in Europe at the present time. It was not, however, the custom in France to name the singers in the programme of the performance; and throughout the eighteenth century no singer in France attained such eminence as was reached by numbers in Italy, where the popularity of the prima donna and the airs she gave herself inspired a satiric writer with words which, to the leading vocalists of the French stage, would have been quite inapplicable.

"The prima donna," says the audacious writer just referred to, "receives ample instructions in her duties both on and off the stage. She is taught how to make engagements and to screw the manager up to exorbitant terms; how to obtain the protection of rash amateurs, who are to attend her at all times, pay her expenses, make her presents, and submit to her caprices. She is taught to be careless at re-hearsals, to be insolent to the other singers, and to perform all manner of musical absurdities on the stage. She must have a music-master to teach her variations, passages, and embellishments to her airs; and some familiar friend, an advocate or a doctor, to show her how to move her arms, turn her head, and use her handkerchief, without telling her why, for that would only confuse her head. She is to endeavour to vary her airs every night; and though the variations may be at cross purposes with the bass, or the violin part, or the harmony of the accompaniments, that matters little, as a modern conductor is deaf and dumb. In her airs and re-citatives in action, she will take care every night to use the same motions of her hand, her head, her fan, and her handkerchief. If she orders a character to be put in chains, and addresses him in an air of rage or disdain, during the symphony she should talk and laugh with him, point out to him people in the boxes, and show how very little she is in earnest. She will get hold of a new passage in rapid triplets, and introduce it in all her airs, quick, slow, lively, or sad ; and the higher she can rise in the scale, the surer she will be of having all the principal parts allotted to her," etc., etc.

French opera-singers were not, in the eighteenth century, particularly well paid; and history relates that Mdlles. Aubry and Verdier, being engaged for the same line of business, had to live in the same room and sleep in the same bed. Nor, as a rule, were they either well educated or well bred.

Mdlle. Desmâtins, the original representative of Armide, was chiefly celebrated for her beauty, her love of good living, her corpulence, and her bad grammar. She is credited with the following letter written after the death of her child : " *Notr anfan ai maure, vien de boneuer, le mien ai de te voire.*" Mdlle. Desmâtins took so much pleasure in representing royal personages that she assumed the (theatrical) costume and demeanour of a queen in her own household, sat on a throne, and made her attendants serve her on their knees. Another vocalist, Marthe le Rochois, accused of grave flirtation with a bassoon, justified herself by showing a promise of marriage which the gallant instrumentalist had written on the back of an ace of spades.

Marthe le Rochois was fond of giving advice to

her companions. "Inspire yourself with the situation," she said to Desmâtins, who had to represent Medea abandoned by Jason; "fancy yourself in the poor woman's place. If you were deserted by a lover whom you adored," added Marthe, thinking, no doubt, of the bassoon, "what would you do?" "I should look for another," replied the ingenuous girl.

But by far the most distinguished operatic actress of this period was Mdlle. de Maupin, now better known through Théophile Gautier's scandalous, but brilliant and vigorously written, novel, than by her actual adventures and exploits ; which, however, were sufficiently remarkable. Among the most amusing of her escapades were her assaults upon Duménil and Thévenard, tenor and baritone of the Académie Royale de Musique. Dressed in male attire, she went up to the former one night in the Place des Victoires, caned him, deprived him of his watch and snuff-box, and the next day produced the trophies at the theatre just as the plundered vocalist was boasting that he had been attacked by three robbers and had put them all to flight. She is said to have terrified the latter to such a degree that he remained for three weeks hiding from her in the Palais Royal.

Mdlle. de Maupin was in many respects the Lola Montes of her day, but with more beauty, more talent, more power, and more daring. When she

appeared as "Minerva," in Lulli's *Cadmus,* and taking
off her helmet to the public, showed all her beautiful
light brown hair, which hung in luxuriant tresses
over her shoulders, the audience were in ecstasies of
delight. With less talent and less power of fascination she would infallibly have been executed for the
numerous fatal duels in which she took part. She
might even have been burnt alive for invading the
sanctity of a convent at Avignon, to say nothing of
her attempting to set fire to it. Perhaps it would be
more correct to say that Lola Montes was the Mdlle.
Maupin of her day—the Maupin of a century which
is moderate in its passions and its vices as in other
things.

Another interesting French singer of the eighteenth century was Madame Favart, chiefly known
in the present day by the popular operetta of which
she is the heroine. This vocalist was for many
years the glory and the chief support of the Opéra
Comique, which, in 1762, combined with the
Comédie Italienne to form but one establishment.
There was so much similarity in the styles culti-
vated at these two theatres, both devoted to
comic opera of the buffo species, that for several
years before the union, Pergolese's *Serva Padrona*
was the favourite piece at one house, *La Servante
Maitresse* (Pergolese's famous work in a French
version) at the other.

One of Madame Favart's greatest admirers was

Marshal Saxe, a brave man, much loved by beautiful women, and especially associated in the present day, thanks to Scribe's interesting drama, with Adrienne Lecouvreur. Maurice de Saxe declares at the end of that play that, whatever reputation he may enjoy in the future, his name will never be mentioned without recalling that of the charming but unfortunate Adrienne. It may be mentioned all the same in connection with Madame Favart.

It is uncertain whether or not the warrior's love for Madame Favart was returned. The Marshal said it was; the lady said it was not; the lady's husband said he didn't know. The best story told about Marshal Saxe and Madame Favart, or rather Mademoiselle Chantilly, which was at that time her name, is one relating to her elopement with Favart from Maestricht during the siege. Mademoiselle Chantilly was a member of the operatic troupe engaged by the Marshal to follow the Army of Flanders, with Favart as director.

Marshal Saxe became deeply enamoured of the young prima donna, and made proposals to her of a nature partly flattering, partly the reverse. She, however, preferred Monsieur Favart, and contrived to escape with him one dark and stormy night. Indeed, so tempestuous was it, that a bridge which formed the communication between the main body of the Army and a corps on the other side of the river was carried away, leaving the detached regiments quite at the mercy of the enemy. The next morning an officer visited the Marshal in his tent and found him in a state of grief and agitation.

"It is a sad affair, no doubt," said the visitor; "but it can be remedied."

"Remedied!" exclaimed the distressed hero; "no, all hope is lost; I am in despair!"

The officer showed that the bridge might be repaired in such and such a manner; upon which, the great commander, whom no military disaster could depress, but who was profoundly afflicted by the loss of a very charming singer, replied:

"Are you talking about the bridge? That can be mended in a couple of hours. I was thinking of Chantilly. Perfidious girl! She has deserted me!"

If it were necessary—if it were even possible—to connect each famous prima donna with some celebrated composer, Sophie Arnould would have to be associated especially with Gluck, in whose operas she achieved her greatest successes. Gluck at this time was in his third style. Every painter, sculptor, or musician, if he lives long enough, is supposed to have three styles; which, if never recognized by himself, are discovered for him by his critics. Gluck's styles may be classed very distinctly; and they correspond, not only with different periods of his life and with the different developments of his talent, but with the different countries for which he wrote. Thus his first style belongs to Italy and his youth; his second to Germany and his middle age; the third to his old age and to France.

Born in 1712, of Bohemian parents and somewhere in Bohemia, Gluck, when he was quite a child, was taught music by his father, himself a musician. Whether his mother was a Czech does not appear. It may be that both parents were of the Czech race; for it was the custom throughout the eighteenth century — the Czech nationality not having yet asserted itself in connection with Panslavism — for the Slavonians of Bohemia to Germanize their names, when, by a simple process of translation, this was possible and easy. Gluck, in any case, was the son of a Bohemian musician, and was taught by his father, when quite a child, to play the violoncello. The boy was, at an early age, left an orphan; but he was already a sufficiently good musician to be able to support himself by playing the violoncello in a wandering company which he now joined. The Bohemian minstrels gradually made their way to Vienna, where the talent of Gluck attracted the attention of some rich and generous connoisseurs, who recognized the youth's genius, and supplied him with the means of completing his musical education. Gluck, according to Handel's well-known dictum, knew no more

of counterpoint than Handel's cook, who must
be supposed to have been unskilled in the art
of setting one note against another, and in part-
writing generally. After studying several years
under Martini, composer of *La Cosa Rara* and
other popular works of the time, Gluck determined to visit Italy, in those days the headquarters of musical art. He went first to Milan
and there produced his first opera on the subject of Artaxerxes. This was so successful that
he was invited to write other works, which were
brought out at Venice, Cremona, and Turin. These
operas were all composed in the Italian style; a
style in which Handel and Hasse also wrote when
they were working for the Italian stage or for
Italian companies.

After some years Gluck had made such a reputation in Italy that his fame gradually extended
to other countries; and in due time he received an
offer from England and was induced to visit
London. Here he had to contend with a formidable rival in the person of Handel. He does not
seem to have been particularly well pleased with
his reception, though at a later period—four years
before his famous visit to Paris—he was prevailed
upon to come to London again. From London
Gluck returned to Vienna and then went on to Italy,
where he produced five new works, all thoroughly
successful. Gluck was by this time regarded by

the Italians as one of their own masters. He wrote
melodiously, and they were satisfied with him. He,
on the other hand, does not seem to have been
satisfied with the Italians; and when he was already
in his forty-seventh year he began to introduce
into his operas more dramatic significance than
they had hitherto presented.

He composed for the Italian Opera of Vienna a
work on the subject of Alcestis; and a second, which
in one form or another was to become celebrated
throughout Europe, on that of Orpheus. On the
occasion of the Emperor Joseph's marriage Gluck
had the distinguished honour of composing a work
in which the principal parts were played by four
Archduchesses and an Archduke; which showed at
least that the Imperial family must have numbered
among its members some good musicians.

Gluck's success in the dramatic line which he had
now adopted went on increasing until one day at
Court a M. du Rollet, attached to the French
Embassy at Vienna, thought the Bohemian maestro
might with advantage compose some works for the
French Opera or Académie Royale, as it was then
called. M. du Rollet was something of a poet, quite
enough to cut a respectable figure as a librettist;
and it may not be altogether cynical to suppose
that his proposition of supplying Gluck with a
" book " was dictated, at least in part, by a wish to
get something of his own performed in association

with so illustrious a master. M. du Rollet in any case prepared for Gluck, and doubtless under his direction, a libretto founded on the *Iphigénie* of Racine. *Iphigénie en Aulide*, once taken in hand by the composer, is said to have been finished for the stage in less than a year. But it is sometimes easier to compose a work than to get it produced; and the French Opera at that time was a close borough into which it was difficult, and for a foreigner almost impossible, to penetrate. Gluck, however, had a powerful friend in Marie Antoinette, wife of the future Louis XVI.; and the amiable Dauphiness assured him that if he came to Paris she would find means to get his *Iphigénie* brought out. Accordingly Gluck went to Paris, taking with him the score of his new work; and things were so managed that within a comparatively short time after his arrival his *Iphigénie* was not only accepted, but, without the ordinary delays on such occasions, put into rehearsal. What could Gluck possibly want in Paris? *Que diable allait il faire dans cette galère?* is a question one can scarcely help asking, taking into account the miserable state at that time of the French Opera.

Writing about the French Opera a few years before Gluck's arrival in Paris, Rousseau represents the singing and the orchestral playing of that establishment as not only deplorable but execrable. Apart from his sneers at French singing and French music generally, Rousseau, in his *Nouvelle Héloise*, puts into the mouth of the hero, St. Preux, a description of the operatic performances at that time presented on the stage of the so-called Académie Royale de Musique. " It must be conceded," writes St. Preux, "that not only all the marvels of nature, but many other marvels, much greater, which no one has ever seen, are represented at great cost at this theatre ; and certainly Pope must have alluded to it when he describes one on which were seen gods, hobgoblins, monsters, kings, shepherds, fairies, fury, joy, fire, a jig, a battle, and a ball." Where Pope's description of so incongruous and monstrous a representation is to be found St. Preux does not tell his correspondent. But Addison, in No. 29 of the *Spectator*, without any " allusion," gives a similar description of the French Opera of which Rousseau, through St. Preux, may have been thinking at the time.

First as to the stage. " Imagine," writes St. Preux, " an inclosure fifteen feet broad and long in proportion. This inclosure is the theatre. On its two sides are placed at intervals screens, on which are grossly painted the objects which the scene is supposed to represent. At the back of the enclosure hangs a great curtain, painted in like manner, and nearly always pierced and torn that it may represent at a little distance gulfs on the earth, or holes in the sky. Everyone who passes behind the stage,

or touches the curtain, produces a sort of earth-
quake, which has a double effect. The sky is made
of certain bluish rags, suspended from poles or
from cords, as linen may be seen hanging out to dry
in any washerwoman's yard. The sun, for it is seen
here sometimes, is a lighted torch in a lantern.
The cars of the gods and goddesses are composed
of four rafters, square and hung on a thick rope in
the form of a swing or see-saw; between the
rafters is a cross plank on which the gods sit down,
and in front hangs a piece of coarse cloth, well
dirtied, which acts the part of clouds for the magnificent cars. One may see, towards the bottom of
the machine, two or three tallow candles, badly
snuffed, which, while the great personage dementedly
presents himself swinging in his see-saw, fumi-
gate him with an incense worthy of his dignity.
The agitated sea is composed of long angular lan-
terns of cloth and blue pasteboard, strung on
parallel spits, which are turned by little black-
guard boys. The thunder is a heavy cart rolled
over an arch, and is not the least agreeable instrument one hears. The flashes of lightning are made
of pinches of resin thrown on a flame, and the thunder is a cracker at the end of a fusee.

"The theatre is, moreover, furnished with little
square traps, which, opening at need, announce that
the demons are about to issue from their cave.
When they have to rise into the air, little demons

of stuffed brown cloth are substituted for them, or sometimes real chimney sweeps, who swing about suspended on ropes till they are majestically lost in the rags of which I have spoken. The accidents, however, which not unfrequently happen, are sometimes as tragic as farcical. When the ropes break, then infernal spirits and immortal gods fall together and lame and occasionally kill one another. Add to all this the monsters, which render some scenes very pathetic, such as dragons, lizards, tortoises, crocodiles, and large toads, who promenade the theatre with a menacing air, and display at the opera all the temptations of St. Anthony. Each of these figures is animated by a lout of a Savoyard, who has not even intelligence enough to play the beast.

"Such, my cousin, is the august machinery of the Opera, as I have observed it from the pit with the aid of my glass; for you must not imagine that all the apparatus is hidden, and produces an imposing effect. I have only described what I have seen myself, and what any other spectator may see. I am assured, however, that there are a prodigious number of machines employed to put the whole spectacle in motion, and I have been invited several times to inspect them; but I have never been curious to learn how little things are performed by great means."

Next as to the music : " You can form no idea of

the frightful cries, the long bellowings, with which
the theatre resounds during the representation!
One sees actresses nearly in convulsions, tearing
yelps and howls violently out of their lungs, closed
hands pressed on their breasts, heads thrown back,
faces inflamed, veins swollen, and stomachs panting.
I know not which of the two, the eye or the ear, is
most agreeably affected by this ugly display ; and,
what is really inconceivable, it is these shriekings
alone that the audience applaud. By the clapping
of their hands they might be taken for deaf people
delighted at catching some shrill, piercing sound.
For my part, I am convinced that they applaud the
outcries of an actress at the Opera as they would
the feats of a tumbler or rope-dancer at a fair.
The sensation produced by this screaming is both
revolting and painful; one actually suffers while it
lasts, but is so glad to see it all over without
accident, as willingly to testify joy. Imagine this
style of singing employed to express the delicate
gallantry and tenderness of Quinault ! Imagine
the muses, the graces, the loves, Venus herself,
using such means of expression, and judge the
effect ! As for devils, it might pass, for this music
has something infernal in it, and is not ill-adapted
to such beings.

" To these exquisite sounds those of the orchestra
are most worthily married. Conceive an endless
charivari of instruments without melody, a drawling

and perpetual rumble of basses, the most lugubrious and fatiguing I have ever heard, and which I have never been able to support for half-an-hour without a violent headache. All this forms a species of psalmody in which there is generally neither melody nor measure. But should a lively air spring up, oh, then, the sensation is universal; you then hear the whole pit in movement, painfully following and with great noise some clever performer in the orchestra. Charmed to feel for a moment a cadence, which they understand so little, their ears, voices, arms, feet, their entire bodies, agitated all over, run after the measure always about to escape them, while the Italians and Germans, who are deeply affected by music, follow it without effort, and never need beat the time. But in this country the musical organ is extremely hard; voices have no softness, their inflections are sharp and strong, and their tones reluctant and forced. There is no cadence, no melodious accents in the airs of the people; their military instruments, their regimental fifes, their horns, and hautboys, their street singers, and guinguette violins, are all so false as to shock the least delicate ear. Talents are not given indiscriminately to all men, and the French seem to me, of all people, to have the least aptitude for music. My Lord Edward says that the English are not better gifted in this respect : but the difference is, that they know it, and do not care about it;

whilst the French would relinquish a thousand just titles to praise, rather than confess that they are not the first musicians in the world."

The French audiences of that time seem to have been worthy of the operatic performances which were expected to interest them; for according to St. Preux, " The French ought not to have a better operatic drama than they possess, at least, as regards execution ; not that they are incapable of appreciating what is good, but because they derive more amusement from what is bad. They feel more gratification in satirizing than in applauding ; the pleasure of criticizing more than compensates them for the *ennui* of witnessing a stupid composition ; and they would rather be able to ridicule a performance after they have left the theatre than enjoy themselves while there."

That Rousseau's criticisms on the French opera, at a time when Sophie Arnould was its principal singer, and just before the arrival of Gluck and Piccinni, did not proceed from a man who was incapable of appreciating Gluck's music, is shown by his " Lettre sur la Musique Française," in which, while praising the melody of the Italians as much as he condemns the psalmody of the French, he expresses the highest admiration for the genius of Gluck. M. Castil Blaze, in his " Molière Musicien," states that Rousseau never missed a representation of *Orphée*. He said, moreover, in reference to the gratification which that work had afforded him, that " after all there was something in life worth living for, since in two hours so much genuine pleasure could be obtained." He had at one time written that good music could never be set to French words ; but he afterwards declared that Gluck seemed to have come to France in order to give the lie to his proposition. At another time he remarked that everyone complained of Gluck's want of melody, but that for his part he thought it " issued from all his pores."

Besides leaving an Opera-house where the company was composed of first-rate artists, for the most part Italians, for one at which the singers, though they may have sung or declaimed with dramatic expression, were by all accounts no vocalists, Gluck made an equally bad exchange as regards the orchestra. On this point, as in regard to the musical execution generally, Dr. Burney is in accord with Rousseau, himself a musician and a composer. The orchestra of the Académie was not only ignorant, but obstinate; and the musicians refused to be taught how to play by a conductor to whose beat they were unaccustomed, a stranger, and, above all, a foreigner.

Gluck possessed a practical knowledge of all the best orchestras in Europe, including, no doubt, some that were not excellent. He had composed works for small as well as large theatres in Italy ;

and he had produced his *Orfeo* in London four years before he went to Paris, where in time he was to bring out this same *Orfeo* with Sophie Arnould in the principal part. But never until he arrived in Paris had it been his ill-fortune to have to entrust orchestral parts to musicians who could not play them. Gradually, however, Gluck subdued those who wished to be his master; and he at the same time increased the number of players and introduced a fitting complement of brass instruments.

If Gluck had to form and train his orchestra, he apparently found a good chorus to work with; and in *Orphée* the chorus-singing was found quite as effective and almost as attractive as the singing of Sophie Arnould in the principal part.

As *Iphigénie*, Sophie Arnould obtained the greatest possible success. The patient and determined composer had rehearsed the work for six months, and had at last got both chorus and orchestra into due subjection. The musicians may be said to have learned under his careful direction the proper use of their instruments. At the first representation of *Iphigénie en Aulide* the Court and the Ministers, with the notable exception of the King and the then reigning favourite, Madame du Barry, were present; and the Dauphin, accompanied by the Dauphiness (Marie Antoinette), the Count and Countess of Provence, the Duchess of Chartres and Bourbon, and the Princess de Lamballe, were admitted into the theatre before the doors were opened. A great disturbance was expected. But Marie Antoinette had requested the Lieutenant of Police to take the necessary precautions; and, although the opera of the evening was the work of a "confounded foreigner," there was no riot.

The charming Sophie distinguished herself by her acting more than by her singing, though she is said to have delivered her melodies as well as her purely dramatic passages with intense expression. Larrivée, who took the part of "Agamemnon," is said by the chroniclers of the time not to have sung through his nose; this abstention on his part being evidently looked upon as something marvellous, or, at least, quite exceptional. Gluck had possibly cured him of his bad habit, which was previously so marked that the people in the pit, who, notwithstanding his grave defect, admired his singing, would say when he had finished one of his airs: "That nose has really a magnificent voice."

Among the singers of the opera, however, the one who really triumphed was Sophie Arnould. Marie Antoinette gave the signal for the applause; and in such a case all the courtiers had to do was to follow. Not only did the Dauphiness encourage Gluck herself, but she visited with severe displeasure all who ventured to treat him disrespectfully. Of this an example occurred in connection with Sophie Arnould. This fascinating woman,

with her sweet voice and her expressive style, had
so subdued the somewhat uncouth composer that
he consented to rehearse *Orphée* in her apartments
instead of — as custom and common sense demanded—at the theatre. At these rehearsals the
musicians attended; and one day when the orchestra
was playing and Sophie Arnould was singing, the
door suddenly opened and in walked the Prince
d'Hennin. This was not one of those final rehearsals in which the singers play their parts as if
before the audience; and Gluck, with all the
principal singers except Sophie Arnould, was sitting down. As the Prince's entry did not cause
them to rise, the conceited nobleman flew into a
rage, and addressing the performing vocalist in the
middle of her air, called out: "It is the custom in
France to rise when anyone enters the room,
especially if it be a person of some consideration."
Gluck, for whom this modest speech was evidently
intended, sprang from his seat and, rushing towards
the intruder, exclaimed : "The custom in Germany
is to rise only for those whom we esteem." Then,
turning to Sophie Arnould, he added : "I see,
Mademoiselle, that you are not mistress in your
own house. I leave you, and shall not set foot
here again."

The overbearing Prince was called to order by
Marie Antoinette herself, who, hearing of his rudeness to Gluck, forced him to beg the composer's

pardon, or, at least, to offer him apologies in some appropriate form. The Prince had to do as he was told ; and he tried to make amends for his incivility by visiting Gluck in person and conveying to him the expression of his regret.

Although Sophie Arnould used to tolerate the Prince d'Hennin and his visits, she had no liking for his society ; and the Count de Lauragais, to whom Sophie was really attached, and who was in the habit of turning the conceited, overbearing Prince into ridicule, arranged at the latter's expense a very elaborate jest. One day when Sophie was unwell and unable to sing, the Count asked her physician whether it would not be necessary to keep up her spirits; and desirable, therefore, to protect her against all depressing influences. The doctor could not but accept the Count's rational suggestion. " Is it not very important, then," continued de Lauragais, "that she should not, in her present state of health, receive visits from the Prince d'Hennin ? " To this the doctor also acceded. But a mere verbal recommendation would not, said the Count, be enough ; and he at last induced the doctor to write, by way of prescription, a formal injunction against visits from the Prince d'Hennin. The Count de Lauragais took possession of this prescription, and forwarded it to the Prince in a polite letter, calling his particular attention to it. The first result was a duel, and the second a violation of the doctor's

orders ; for the same evening the Count so solici-
tous about Sophie Arnould's health, and the Prince
whose presence had been declared, on high medical
authority, an obstacle to her convalescence, met at
the patient's house.

But Gluck was firm, and the rehearsals of *Orphée*
now took place at the theatre, where it became the
fashion for people of the Court, and all who had the
entry, to attend them.

The opera in which Sophie Arnould next
appeared was the rearrangement—of course with
a French libretto—of the *Alcestis*, which Gluck had
already given at Vienna ; as he had given *Orphée*
at Vienna, in various Italian cities, and in London.

When, four years after Gluck's arrival in Paris,
Piccinni was sent for by Madame du Barry in order
to extinguish the composer favoured by Marie
Antoinette, he saw—as Gluck had seen before him—
that the French had no vocalists ; and when one
evening he met Gluck at a supper given in honour
of the rival composers, he said to him : " The
French are a strange people. They wish us to write
operas for them and they cannot sing." Piccinni
was, in his way, as great a composer as Gluck, and
he aided the progress of opera by the development he gave to the concerted finale. He was
treated with no injustice in Paris ; and ₅in the
literary warfare to which the presence of an Italian
and German composer in Paris gave rise, he had as

many and as influential partisans as his rival.
Marie Antoinette, who, as a Viennese, could not dislike Italian music, had made no objection whatever
to his visit nor to the appointment which he received.
But Gluck with his strong nature took pleasure in
strife, or, at least, was in no way disheartened by it;
whereas Piccinni could not struggle with obstacles
or with disapprobation, and he fled from Paris when
in spite, or perhaps in consequence, of the most
determined opposition from the Gluckists (though
never from Gluck himself), he was about to obtain
a brilliant success.

Of Sophie Arnould's performance in Gluck's
Armide the chroniclers of the period say nothing.
The work was not liked, though it is now classed
(together with *Orphée* or *Orfeo* and the second
Iphigénie) among his finest works. Gluck himself
had made sure that his *Armide* would prove a great
success. To Marie Antoinette's question as to
whether *Armide* was finished, and how he liked it,
Gluck, according to Madame Campan, calmly replied: " Madame, il est bientôt fini, et vrainent ce sera
superbe." Otto Jahn, in his excellent " Life of
Mozart," explains the failure of *Armide* partly by
the " dangerous rivalry of Lulli," who, however, if he
had lived until the production of Gluck's *Armide* at
Paris, would by that time have been nearly one hundred and fifty years old. Herr Jahn means of course
that *Armide* suffered from the dangerous rivalry of

Lulli's operas, which, however, had ceased to be performed. Gluck is known to have studied them carefully in order to be able, in setting French words, to accommodate himself to the French taste.

Sophie Arnould, like Mademoiselle de Maupin, Adrienne Lecouvreur, Madame Favart, and other eminent French actresses, lyrical or purely dramatic, has been made the leading figure in a work of fiction : a play, or vaudeville, in her case, which has for its subject the abduction of Sophie from her home, and the inscription of her name on the books of the French Opera. Once registered on the list of persons engaged at the Académie Royale de Musique, a young woman, of however tender an age, was freed from all control on the part of her family. She was her own, or anyone else's mistress ; and as long as she obeyed the rules of the establishment which had taken possession of her, was answerable to no one for her actions. A young girl might go of her own accord to the Opera, or be persuaded to present herself there ; or, as sometimes happened, her name might be entered on the books by another person, who had previously, perhaps, decoyed her from the custody of her parents. In none of these cases had her family any further power over her. *Lettres de cachet* might even be issued, commanding the persons named therein to join the Opera ; and it was in this way that the Count de Melun, an

unscrupulous admirer of the two demoiselles de
Camargo, got both of them assigned to the ballet
department of the Académie. Another profligate
patron of the Opera, the Duke de Fronsac, sinned
in like manner, and was reproved in indignant
verses by Gilbert, the unhappy author of the famous
poem: "Au banquet de la vie infortuné convive," &c.
Here are the lines on the subject of the Duke de
Fronsac's offence :—

> Qu'on la séduise. Il dit : ses eunuques discrets,
> Philosophes abbés, philosophes valets,
> Intriguent, sément l'or, trompent les yeux d'un père ;
> Elle cède, on l'enlève : en vain gémit sa mère.
> Echue à l'Opèra par un rapt solennel,
> Sa honte la dérobe au pouvoir paternal.

The tyranny practised in connection with the
Opera was by no means confined to young women.
Male amateurs, the beauty of whose voices had been
remarked, were sometimes forced to take engagements at the Académie ; and more than one abbé is
said to have had his talent diverted from an ecclesi-
astical to a lyrical career. All pupils and associates
of the Académie enjoyed special privileges, including
(as already set forth) absolute freedom from parental
restraint. The persons, moreover, of singers, dancers, and musicians belonging to the Opera were
exempt from liability to seizure for debt.

In France, it may be added, during the eighteenth
century, it was not the custom for young ladies in
good society to visit the Opera before their mar-

riage; though, once attended by a husband, the
newly-wedded girl could show herself there as
much as she pleased. It was, indeed, a point of
etiquette that through the Opera she should make
her entrance into fashionable life. These *débutantes*
of the audience department presented themselves to
the public in their richest attire, their most brilliant
diamonds; and, if the effect was good, the gentlemen in the pit testified their approbation by clapping their hands. After a time, towards the end of
the reign of Louis XV., brevets conferring the
rights and privileges of married ladies on single ones
were introduced. Any young girl who held a *brevet
de dame* could present herself at the Opera, which
in the absence of such a brevet would have been
practically impossible. "The number of these brevets," says Bachaumont, in the "Mémoires Secrètes,"
"increased prodigiously under Louis XVI., and very
young persons have been known to obtain them.
Thus removed from the modesty, simplicity, and
retirement of the virginal state, they give themselves
up with impunity to all sorts of scandals. Such
disorder has opened the eyes of the Government;
and it is now only by the greatest favour that one of
the brevets can be obtained."

The Court choir had its system of conscription
equally with the Académie Royale de Musique; and
it was on the list of the King's choristers that
Sophie Arnould's name was inscribed before, by an

easy transition, she was made to pass from the
Chapel Royal to the Opera House. The Princess
of Modena had heard Mademoiselle Arnould at
the Val de Grâce, "whither," says a trustworthy
historian, "her Royal Highness had retired, according to the fashion of the time, to atone, during a
portion of Lent, for the sins she had committed
during the Carnival, and where she chanced to hear
a young girl singing a vesper hymn. The Princess
spoke of Mademoiselle Arnould's talents at the
Château; and in spite of her mother's opposition
(the parents kept a lodging-house somewhere in
Paris), she was inscribed on the list of choristers at
the King's chapel. Madame de Pompadour, already
struck by the beauty of her eyes, which are said to
have been enchantingly expressive, exclaimed, when
she heard her sing: 'Il y à la de quoi faire une
princesse.'"

Sophie Arnould owed her pretty name, in part at
least, to her own good taste, and in no way to her
godfathers and godmothers, who christened her
Anne Madeleine. Born 1748, in the very room
where Admiral Coligny was assassinated, she used
to say of her arrival in this world: "Je suis venue
au monde par une porte célèbre." She remained
but a short time in the King's choir, and in the
year 1761, being just thirteen years of age, she
made her *début* at the Opera. It is matter of
authentic record that she wore on that occasion a

lilac dress embroidered in silver. Her talent, combined with her wonderful beauty, ensured her success ; and before she had been a fortnight on the stage all Paris was in love with her. When she was announced to sing, the doors of the Opera were besieged by such crowds that Fréron, the chroniqueur, expressed a doubt whether people would give themselves so much trouble to enter Paradise. She is said to have sung " with a limpid and melodious voice," and to have acted with " all the grace and sentiment of a practised *comédienne*." Garrick, visiting Paris, saw her and heard her sing; and he afterwards declared that she was " the only actress on the French stage who had really touched his heart."

The fascinating Sophie was as witty as she was beautiful, and her *mots* were repeated by all the fashionable poets and philosophers of Paris. Her suppers became celebrated, but her life of amusement did not cause her to forget the Opera. As an instance of the effect her singing had upon the public, it may be mentioned that when one evening she refused to appear on the stage and took her seat among the audience, saying that she had come to take a lesson from her rival, Mademoiselle Laguerre, the Minister to whose department the management of the Opera belonged did not venture to do more than reprimand her, though the directors had demanded her imprisonment at Fort l'Evêque.

Not only the directors, but also the public had taken offence, and a party was formed to hiss her on the night following her escapade. But no sooner did she begin to sing than the conspirators felt themselves disarmed, and those who had come to hiss remained to applaud.

Sophie Arnould and her rival, Mademoiselle Laguerre, used both to sing in the operas of Gluck and of Piccinni. If, then, it is true that Gluck once said to Piccinni, at the famous supper party at which the two great composers came together, that the " French were strange people, wanting operas written for them when they were unable to sing," it must be doubted whether either of them can be looked upon as a vocalist. It will be remembered that it was Sophie's histrionic, not her vocal, talent that charmed Garrick. She was " the only actress," he said, not "the only singer" who had really touched his heart. It was, perhaps, because she had never studied the art of vocalization in a good school that her vocal powers gave way before their time. She was only twenty-seven years of age when the Gluck and Piccinni contests began, and already the dilapidated condition of her voice was considered a fair subject of jest. The Abbé Galiani said of her that she had " the finest asthma he had ever heard." It is true that at this time the sarcasms exchanged between Gluckists and Piccinnists had their origin

chiefly in the spirit of partisanship by which each
side was animated. If the singing voice of Sophie
Arnould was to the Abbé Galiani nothing but an
asthma, that of Mademoiselle Lesueur had no effect
on the ears of Marmontel but to " tear " them.
" Mademoiselle," he observed (when Mademoiselle
Lesueur, in Gluck's *Alceste*, had just exclaimed " Il
me déchire le cœur "), " Mademoiselle, vous me
déchirez les oreilles."

" What a lucky thing for you," replied the Abbé
Arnaud, one of the few literary men who took part
with Gluck, " if you could get new ones."

Sophie Arnould, one of the wittiest women who
ever lived, contributed her share of sharp things to
the collection since made of *mots* relating to the
Gluck and Piccinni controversy. Avoiding, however, the æsthetic question, she confined herself to
attacking her rival, Mademoiselle Laguerre. On
one occasion when Mademoiselle Laguerre was
playing the part of the heroine in Piccinni's
Iphigenia in Tauris (the competing composers had
worked on the same libretto), Sophie Arnould, sitting in the audience department, saw the daughter
of Agamemnon reeling about the stage in the most
unbecoming manner.

" Ah," said Sophie, " this is not *Iphigenia in
Tauris ;* this is *Iphigenia in champagne.*"

Madeleine Guimard, the chief ballerina at the
Opera where Sophie Arnould held the post of

principal singer, was as thin as Sarah Bernhardt in
the present day is said to be. Sophie Arnould
called her " La squelette des Grâces ; " and one
evening, when, in a *pas de trois*, she was playing
the part of a nymph between two Fauns, Sophie
said that the two male dancers, Vestris and Dor-
beval, contending for the possession of so meagre a
prize reminded her of two dogs fighting for a bone.

One of Madeleine Guimard's warmest admirers
was Monseigneur de Jarente, titular bishop of
Orleans, who held " la feuille des bénéfices," and
frequently disposed of them in accordance with the
suggestion of his young friend. " Ce petit ver à
soie," said Sophie, "devrait être plus gras. Elle
mange une si bonne feuille."

One day, when Bernard, Rameau's librettist-in-
ordinary, was at a house uttering apparently meaningless words, Sophie asked him what he was
saying.

" I was talking to myself," he answered.

" Take care," she replied ; " you are conversing
with a flatterer."

Another time she said, when Madeleine Guimard
was dancing, " Il n'est pas nécessaire d'aller à Saint
Cloud pour voir jouer les eaux (les os)."

Being told that a capuchin had been eaten by
wolves, she exclaimed : " Poor beasts, what a dreadful thing hunger must be ! "

In 1789, the year of the Revolution, she was

obliged to sell her beautiful villa ; and she purchased, four years afterwards, the Presbytére of Clignancourt, which had belonged to a community of Franciscan monks. Having now finished her life of gaiety, she placed over the entrance to the ancient religious house the inscription "Ite, missa est." In thus adopting for her motto the last words of the mass she did not altogether jest, for she seems about this time to have had serious ideas of becoming religious in her old age ; but she met with a priest who inspired her with so much dislike that she changed her mind. In reference to this she used to say that the unfortunate ecclesiastic "lost the chance of making a good convert."

Helvetius, Diderot, Jean Jacques Rousseau and Voltaire were among those who congregated at her assemblies ; for in those days philosophers and actresses seem to have come together by mutual attraction. Thus when the celebrated dancer, Mademoiselle Sallé, visited London, Fontenelle thought it quite natural to give her a letter of introduction to Locke. The French wit, moreover, may have been struck by the obvious connection between legs and the "human understanding." Lightminded philosophers were not the only ones who found delight in Sophie's society ; for Benjamin Franklin, when he was on his famous mission to Paris, underwent, like so many other men of distinction, her irresistible charm. The conquests of the siren would not, indeed, have been complete had she failed to subjugate the Quaker. One day, when Voltaire was accusing himself of past sins, he went on to say:

" I am eighty-four years old, Mademoiselle, and I have committed eighty-four follies."

" I am not yet forty," replied Sophie, " and I have committed more than a thousand."

She wished to be classed with the Ninons of France, the Aspasias of Greece; and apart from her desire to have her praises sounded in immortal verse she had a genuine taste for literature. It was by pretending to be a poet that the Chevalier de Lauragais (who was really a poetaster of some merit) first made her acquaintance; thus anticipating the device resorted to with a like object by " Francis I." in *Le Roi S'anuise*, and by his musical equivalent, the " Duke of Manhua," in *Rigoletto*.

Of a singer whose voice was marked by vulgarity, and who, naturally enough, met with no success, Sophie said : " Elle a cependant la voix du peuple."

To another who was very pretty, but unable to speak her own language, and who complained that she was overwhelmed by the number of her admirers, she observed : " It would be so easy to get rid of them. You have only to speak."

Meeting one day in the country a doctor who was carrying a gun, and who was about to visit a patient:

" And are you really afraid," she said, looking at the
fowling-piece, " that the poor man will escape you ? "

She showed herself a match even for that master
of wit and satire, Beaumarchais. The author of the
Marriage of Figaro had just brought out at the
Théâtre Français a very dull piece called *Les deux
amis,* and he was telling Sophie Arnould that he
was afraid that night there would be no people at
the Opera. " Vos deux amis nous en enverront," she
replied.

Seeing the portraits of Sully and Choiseul on the
same snuff-box (though why they should have been
thus placed together it is difficult to understand),
she said in reference to the wise economy of the one,
the extravagance of the other : " C'est la recette et
la dépense."

Mademoiselle Laguerre, by the way, was to Sophie
Arnould much what Henry IV.'s famous Minister
was to the spendthrift Choiseul.   The former realized
an immense fortune ; the latter found herself in her
old age nearly destitute.

Without being constant, Sophie Arnould seems
to have been faithful; and it was not her fault if
the most assiduous of her admirers after an intimacy
of four years broke off all connection with her.
Strictly speaking, he was quite right in doing so ;
for, apart from other considerations, he was a
married man. But it was in no virtuous fit that
the Count de Lauragais separated from Sophie.   He

had found a new passion, and this becoming known to Mademoiselle Arnould she would have nothing more to say to him. More than that, she sent to the Countess de Lauragais everything she had received from the Count—laces, ornaments of various kinds, boxes of jewellery, a carriage, and two children. Not to be outdone in generosity by the actress, the countess, with as much kindness as good taste, kept the two children, but returned the carriage, the jewellery, the ornaments, and the lace.

It matters little why the Count de Lauragais quarrelled with Sophie. All that can be recorded in his favour is that he paid a large sum of money to the Opera in order to obtain the abolition of the seats on the stage. Previously, the *habitués* of the theatre had been in the habit of crowding the stage to such an extent that an actor was sometimes obliged to request the public to open a way for him before he could make his entry. In his relations with Sophie Arnould the Count seems to have been furiously, madly jealous; and this jealousy was doubtless one of the determining causes of her separating from him. He is said, however, to have formed an attachment about the time of the separation for a very pretty *débutante* in the ballet department. Questioned by Sophie Arnould as to what progress he was making in his suit, he admitted that he was not getting on; and he added that whenever he called upon the young woman he

found a certain knight of Malta in her rooms. "Il
est là pour chasser les infidèles," said Sophie.

Due allowance being made for the circumstances
in which she was placed, it can scarcely be said that
the witty, genial, kind-hearted Sophie Arnould was
vicious; and of the numerous writers whom she
has interested, none accuse her of having given the
Count de Lauragais any cause for his jealous fits.
She appears to have been naturally of a romantic
disposition; and it has been justly said that a
tendency to romance, though it may mislead a girl,
yet does not deprave her. During her last illness, in
narrating to her confessor the unedifying story of
her life, she had to speak of the terrible jealousy of
the Count de Lauragais, whom, in spite of everything, she had really loved.

"My poor child, how much you must have
suffered," said the benevolent priest. " Ah, c'était
le bon temps, j'étais si malheureuse ! " replied
Sophie.

It is difficult to think of Sophie Arnould without
calling to mind her associate during so many years,
Madeleine Guimard, whose walls, in her magnificent,
luxuriously furnished hotel, were painted by
Fragonard and by Louis David; whose foot was
moulded by Houdin, the famous sculptor; and for
whose arm, which a "too, too solid" cloud falling
from the theatrical heaven had unhappily broken,
a mass was said in the church of Notre Dame.

Fragonard, introducing in most of his mural pictures the face and figure of the local goddess, is said at last not only to have fallen in love with her, which she might have overlooked, but to have given signs of jealousy, which she could not tolerate. It was then that David, afterwards to become celebrated under the Republic, and under the Empire, was called in. The severe, classically minded young artist could not have found in the decoration of Madeleine Guimard's "Temple of Terpsichore," as she called her home, very congenial work; and perceiving this to be the case, the generous woman gave him the sum he was to have received for covering her walls with fantastic designs, and left him free to continue his studies and do his work elsewhere and according to his own ideas.

For Madeleine Guimard was considerate as well as charitable. This she again showed in her conduct during the severe winter of 1768, when she visited all the houses of the poor in her own neighbourhood, and gave to each destitute family enough to live on for a year. It was then that Marmontel, deeply affected by her generosity and kindheartedness, addressed to her the famous epistle beginning " Est il bien vrai, jeune et belle damnée?" &c. " Not yet Magdalen repentant" (her name, it will be remembered, was Madeleine), "but already Magdalen charitable!" exclaimed a priest in his sermon; for although Mademoiselle Guimard had

herself said nothing about it, the fame of her
generosity had now spread through Paris. "The
hand," continued the preacher, "which knows so
well how to give alms will not be rejected by St.
Peter when it knocks at the gates of Paradise."

With all her powers of fascination, the "jeune et
belle damnée" of Marmontel's verse was not beautiful; and her extreme thinness caused her to be
called familiarly among her companions *l'araignée.*
This recalls Byron's remarks about thin women, who
reminded him, if ugly of spiders, if pretty of dried
butterflies. Madeleine Guimard was certainly not
ugly; and, with or without beauty, she exercised
upon those around her the effect that beauty
exercises. She is said at a comparatively advanced
age to have preserved in a marvellous manner
the appearance of youth, and she possessed such a
perfect acquaintance with all the mysteries of the
toilet that " by the art of dress and adornment alone
she could have made herself look young when she
was clearly beginning to grow old." Queen Marie
Antoinette used to consult her about her dress and
the arrangement of her hair; and once when, for
some act of rebellion at the Opera, she had been
ordered to Fort l'Evêque, she is said to have consoled her maid, the companion of her captivity, by
saying to her : " Never mind, I have written to the
Queen to tell her that I have discovered a new style
of coiffure. We shall be free before the evening."

M. Arsène Houssaye, in his " Galerie du dixhui-
tième Siècle," tells us that, towards 1780, Madeleine
Guimard began to lose her popularity : " Vers 1780
elle tomba peu à peu dans l'oubli." In 1789, the
year of the taking of the Bastille, she visited
London. At such a time a Parisian artist might
well think it opportune to make a foreign tour; and
as a matter of fact, a number of French dancers
came to London, with Madeleine Guimard among
them. Lord Mount Edgcumbe saw her dance at the
King's Theatre (Her Majesty's in the present day),
and describes her, in his " Musical Reminiscences,"
as "full of grace and gentility," adding that she
"had never possessed more." He also tells us that
she was " now sixty years of age," though, as a
matter of fact, having been born in 1737, she was
only fifty-two. This tendency to exaggerate the
age of artists who have long been before the
public may often be noticed.

After her return to Paris Madeleine Guimard appeared for the last time, in 1796, at a special performance for the benefit of aged and retired artists.
Times were bad ; her aristocratic friends were in
exile, or had fallen beneath the guillotine ; and she
had returned to her own rich and influential pro-
tector, the Prince de Soubise, the pension he had
formerly assigned to her. Soubise's son-in-law, the
Prince de Guéméné, had contracted debts to the
amount of forty million francs, and the heads of

the family having decided that the time had come for them to economize, and even to make sacrifices for the benefit of the spendthrift's three thousand creditors, the Prince, in whom Madeleine Guimard was strongly interested, absented himself from the Opera, and gave no longer to his *protégées* the *petits soupers* for which he had been celebrated.

Thereupon a number of the *danseuses* assembled in Madeleine Guimard's room and drew up the following kindly-meant letter to their generous friend :—

" MY LORD,

" Accustomed to see you amongst us at the performances of the Opera, we have noticed with the most bitter regret that you not only deprive yourself of the pleasure of the representations, but also that none of us are now asked to the little suppers you used so often to give, and at which we had, turn by turn, the happiness of interesting you. Rumour has informed us only too truly of the reason of your seclusion and of your just grief. Hitherto we have feared to trouble you, sacrificing sensibility to respect. Nor should we, even now, venture to break silence without an imperious motive, which our delicacy can no longer resist.

" We had flattered ourselves, my lord, that the Prince de Guéméné's bankruptcy—to make use of a term which is repeated in the coffee-houses, the clubs, the journals of France, and elsewhere—would not be so considerable, so enormous as was said beforehand; and above all, that the wise precautions taken by the King to assure the claimants the amount of their debts, and to avoid expenses and depredations—more potent than even the insolvency itself—would not disappoint general expectation. But affairs are evidently in such disorder that there is no longer any hope. So we judge, from the generous sacrifices to which the heads of your illustrious house, following your example, have resigned themselves. We should consider ourselves guilty of ingratitude, my lord, did we not imitate you in your considerateness—did we not return to you the pensions which your munificence has lavished upon us. Apply these revenues, my lord, to the relief of so many retired officers, so many poor men of letters, so many unfortunate domestics whom the Prince de Guémené drags with him into ruin.

" For ourselves we have other resources, and we shall have lost nothing, my lord, if we retain your esteem. We shall even have gained if, by refusing your gifts now, we compel our detractors to admit that we were not unworthy of them.

" We are, with profound respect, my lord, your Serene Highness's very humble and devoted servants, GUIMARD, HEINEL," etc., — with twenty other names.

Sophie Arnould had fared under the Revolution as badly as Madeleine Guimard. At one moment she seems to have been in danger of her life. She was actually accused of " aristocratic tendencies." " If I did not sympathize with the Republic should I keep the bust of Marat in my room?" she replied, pointing at the same time to a bust of Gluck.

The chronicle of the French Opera-house reintroduces her to us in connection with that very representation for the benefit of " aged and retired artists," in which, as already mentioned, Madeleine Guimard took part. Among the various amateurs who had come to see Madeleine Guimard dance for the last time, now that she was really in her sixtieth year, was an old *habitué* dating from the reign of Louis XV., who, after the performance, called a coach, drove home, and was proceeding to pay the driver when the latter called out :

" Who ever heard of the Count de Lauragais paying the Chevalier de Ferrières for taking him home in his carriage ? "

" What ! is it you ? " asked Lauragais.

" Myself," answered Ferrières.

The two old friends embraced one another, and the Chevalier then told the Count that when all the Royalists were either concealing themselves or emigrating he had done both. Disguised in the great-coat of his coachman, he had emigrated to the Boulevard, and in the character of the driver of a public vehicle (he had, of course, painted out the coat-of-arms on the panels) had passed unrecognized through the Reign of Terror.

The Count de Lauragais insisted now on driving home the Chevalier de Ferrières; and their journeys and return journeys might have occupied some considerable time had it not been finally arranged that the two friends should meet the next morning at Sophie Arnould's. Fouché, who in former days had been desperately in love with her, pitied her in her distress; and he had obtained for her, on the part of the State, an apartment and a pension of two thousand four hundred francs, as "a national reward for the eminent services rendered by the *citoyenne* Arnould to the country and to the sovereign people at the Opera."

Thanks to Sophie's influence with the Minister of Police, the Chevalier received an order authorizing him to return to France, though, it is said, he had never left Paris except occasionally to drive a fare to one of the suburbs.

CHAPTER VI.

MARA.

GERMANY has been the birth-place of but few of the
prime donne who have attained celebrity throughout Europe, though exception must be made in the
striking cases of Madame Mara and of Mademoiselle
Sontag. Gertrude Elizabeth Mara, one of the most
brilliant and most famous vocalists of the latter part
of the eighteenth century, was born to the name of
Schmäling, and her father was a musician of good
repute at Hesse Cassel. Soon after her birth in
February, 1749, she had the misfortune to lose her
mother; and, like the Ursule Mirouet of Balzac, she
was brought up by her father, who bestowed upon
her at once paternal and maternal care. Herr
Schmäling, when he was not playing in the orchestra,
occupied himself with repairing musical instruments,
and especially violins. In her father's absence Fraülein Schmäling used to make experiments with the
violins, and in executing a pizzicato she one day
snapped a string. On her parent's return she was

well scolded and she doubtless promised never to touch the violins again. But once more she committed the fault for which she had already been severely reproved, and this time Herr Schmäling determined not to let off his peccant daughter so easily as before.

"There is only one punishment," he said, " appropriate to your offence and for your persistence in touching my violins. I will make you a violinist."

The child laughed at this grotesque threat, and, taking up a violin and a bow, showed that she was already something of a player. Under her father's tuition she studied assiduously, and rapidly became an excellent violinist.

Among other prime donne who began their musical studies by learning to play the violin may be mentioned Madame Christine Nilsson.

Soon the fame of the youthful prodigy became spread through the neighbourhood. The little girl was invited out that she might display her wonderful talents to admiring guests, and on these occasions she received handsome presents. Fraülein Schmäling was now six years of age, and already old enough, it was thought, to play in public. Accordingly her father took her out on a touring expedition, first visiting Frankfort, where the infant phenomenon played with great success, and afterwards making their way through the Rhine cities to the Dutch frontier. After "doing" Holland the father and daughter crossed over to England. Fraülein Schmäling had by this time become quite a big girl. She was ten years old, and we may be sure had a demeanour beyond her age. In London she was warmly received, and was invited to play before King George III. During her stay in London the future prima donna seems to have made her first essays in singing; and, before she left, her father placed her under an Italian vocalist of good reputation, Signor Paradisi. The Italian proposed an arrangement, common enough in the present day, by which, in return for his instruction, he was to receive for a term of years half his pupil's salary. Herr Schmäling, however, would not accept these conditions. The negotiations with Signor Paradisi were broken off, and for want of a better instructor the violinist resolved to teach his little daughter himself.

Meanwhile the little Schmäling had ceased to be a violinist, and as she could not yet appear in public as a singer, the father, who had partly counted upon her for ways and means, found himself in a very difficult position. At last he was reduced to such straits that he was obliged to take to street performances. He played the flute, while to the accompaniment of the guitar his daughter sang. Strolling from town to town the wandering musicians at last reached Wells, where they had the good fortune to be heard by a great lover

of music, Dr. Harrington. The doctor was charmed
by the little girl's voice, and distressed to hear
that the father had been reduced by ill-fortune to the necessity of earning his bread in the
character of musical vagrant. He gave Herr
Schmäling an introduction to some friends at Bath,
begging them to help the bearer in getting up a concert. This, when his daughter's voice had once been
heard, proved no difficult matter, and when all the
necessary preliminary arrangements had been made
Dr. Harrington arrived from Wells to see that at the
last moment nothing was wanting. The concert
proved thoroughly successful, and yielded enough
money to enable the Schmälings to regain their
native land.

At Cassel Schmäling learned that Frederick the
Great had just formed a musical establishment at
Berlin, in which he determined at once to seek an
engagement for himself and daughter. Frederick,
however, who wrote in French and sang in Italian,
and who regarded his fellow countrymen as bar-
barians in matters of art, would not believe that a
good singer could come out of Germany. Schmäling's application was received then very coldly;
but the young girl had arranged to give a concert
at Berlin, and the King sent his principal singer,
Morelli, to hear her and see what she was worth.
" She sings like a German," was the Italian's brief
but damnatory report. Frederick could not endure

the singing of Germans, and neither the young Elizabeth nor her father was engaged.

In 1766 father and daughter went to Leipsic, where they gave a concert under the direction of Hiller, a musical name for which new celebrity was to be gained in our own century. Here the child— she was now seventeen—met with success, and an engagement was offered to her at the Opera-house. She was to take principal parts, but the salary assigned to her would have been thought contemptible in the present day. During her stay at Leipsic, Fraülein Schmäling studied the harpsichord —precursor of the pianoforte, at that time not invented—and soon afterwards she was sufficiently mistress of the instrument to be able to play with marked success at several concerts. The accomplished young vocalist and musician is said to have been far from good-looking. She was short in stature, was wanting in demeanour, had irregular and projecting teeth ; but, at the same time, an expression in her countenance of amiability and good humour. She was very agreeable, too, in conversation. As an actress, she seems to have been indifferent.

With unquestionably defects, to hear her sing was to forget them all. She had a compass of nearly three octaves, extending in the upper register to the higher E. She combined sweetness with power, and her singing was as remarkable for fluency and volubility as for intensity of expression. Violinist and pianist as well as vocalist, she could read the most difficult music at sight—a talent not possessed by many singers of that day. The training of the voice was at that time considered of more importance than a general knowledge of music. From Leipsic, Saxony's chief commercial city, Fraülein Schmäling went to Dresden, its famous capital. The Grand Duke of Saxony had heard her on the occasion of a visit to the Leipsic Fair; and so highly did he think of her that he invited her to give a series of performances at Dresden. As a child, before her talents were mature, little Elizabeth had, probably without much emotion, and with the unconsciousness of a child, sung before George III. To sing, however, in the character of a finished vocalist before the Court of Dresden was now a more serious matter; and the young artist was so nervous that the Grand Duchess had to give her much kind encouragement before she could feel at her ease.

Italy was still at this time the musical centre of Europe, and especially for opera; nor was Frederick the Great the only amateur who held that in Italy alone could the art of singing be acquired.

The young German vocalist was anxious, however, to make her mark at Berlin; the more so, perhaps, because her first endeavour in that direction had so signally failed. She was now twenty-two years of age and her voice was well developed. She had been a musician all her life, and in applying for an engagement at Berlin, where an Italian Opera-house was now established, she felt sure that, were she but allowed an opportunity of appearing, she would from the first moment carry the public with her. A hundred years ago Italian was the recognized language of opera wherever performed. This, however, as in the present day, did not exclude composers and singers who were not Italians from making themselves heard in connection with Italian companies. Handel, for instance, composed numbers of Italian operas; and Italian was the language in which Hasse's works were written and in which Madame Schmäling, appearing in them, sang for the first time at Berlin. Frederick still thought that there could be nothing in her, it being his fixed belief that one might as well look for musical playing in the neighing of a horse as in the singing of a German.

But the success of the new comer with the Berlin public was complete. She was applauded with enthusiasm, and so great was the excitement caused by her performances that the King at last began to think there must be something in her. He accordingly sent her from Potsdam an invitation to the Palace.

Frederick II., besides being a flute player (though Quantz, his professor, declares that he was but a poor executant), was also a composer; and he himself directed the performances at the Opera-house he had established. The chief aim of this despotic musical conductor was to make the singers keep to their parts, instead of wandering from them according to the custom of vocalists in all ages under pretext of adorning them.

He was as severe, too, with the orchestral players as with the singers; and the stick which he wielded, after the manner of our modern conductors long before the use of the orchestral *bâton* had been introduced, was occasionally used as an instrument not only of guidance, but also of correction.

Fraülein Schmäling was introduced into the King's presence. Frederick for a time remained silent. Instead of showing any signs of the confusion which in some degree she must have felt, the young vocalist walked about the room examining the pictures.

At last Frederick, who was sitting down, invited her to approach, and on her coming towards him asked her what she proposed to sing. She sat down at the harpsichord, and, without waiting for instructions, began one of her favourite airs. The King was much struck by the performance; but he maintained an attitude of reserve. Then he asked whether she could sing at sight, and placing before her a difficult bravura called upon her to begin it. She sang it to perfection; and after trying her in another piece the musical Monarch gave in. He complimented the young artist warmly, begged her to sing again, and at last dismissed her with a valuable token of his admiration.

Every day the German vocalist who sang like an Italian had now to visit Potsdam, and on leaving Berlin she took with her a formal engagement for the following year. Her salary for the season was a very moderate one, equivalent to about £450. Frederick, however, is known to have loved both order and economy, and he paid out of his own purse the entire expenses of his operatic establishment.

At Berlin Fraülein Schmäling made the acquaintance of a violoncellist named Mara, a *protégé* of the King's brother, Prince Henry; a gentleman of showy appearance and impressive manners, who had not much trouble in persuading the rising vocalist to become his wife. Frederick, seeing what was going on, endeavoured to prevent this misfortune, as, to Fraülein Schmäling, he knew it must prove; for Mara had, together with other defects, loose morals and an ungovernable temper. Before getting married it was necessary to obtain the King's permission, and this was sternly refused. Under these circumstances the lovers eloped, but they were soon captured and brought back as prisoners to Berlin. The sentence passed upon Mara was of a highly grotesque kind. He was made a fifer in an infantry regiment at Kustrin. But the

period of Mara's fifing was soon at an end. He was
allowed to return to Berlin, and more than that was
permitted to marry Fraülein Schmäling.

The charming Elizabeth had not long been
married when she found that Frederick's paternal
warnings had not been addressed to her without
cause. More than once her husband struck her;
and at last, in a moment of alcoholic excitement, he
not only beat her in a general way, but ended by
blackening one of her eyes. The conduct of the
ruffian 'cellist could no longer be concealed from
the King, before whom, by reason of her discoloured
eye, Madame Mara declared herself unable to
appear. Frederick summoned the brutal husband
to his presence and told him that since he was so
fond of beating he had better once more enter a
regimental band, where, this time, he would beat
the drum. Mara tapped the parchment for a
month, and was then allowed to return to his
wife.

When, in 1780, Madame Mara and her husband
wished to visit England the King positively prohibited their departure, and on their escaping to
Vienna, sent a dispatch to the Emperor, Joseph
II., requesting him to arrest the fugitives and send
them back. The Emperor, however, merely gave
them a hint that they had better leave Vienna as
soon as possible ; when he would inform the King
that his messenger had arrived too late. Afterwards,

as soon as it was thought she could becomingly
do so, Madame Mara made her appearance at the
Vienna Opera, and sang there with great success
for nearly two years.

According to another version of Madame Mara's
flight, she was arrested before she had passed the
Prussian frontier, and separated from her husband,
who was shut up in a fortress, and, instead of performing on the violoncello in the orchestra of the
Opera, was made once more to play the drum in
a regiment. The tears of the singer had no effect
upon the inflexible Monarch, and it was only by
giving up a portion of her salary (so, at least,
runs this anecdote of dubious authenticity) that
she could obtain Herr Mara's liberation.

It is certain that the position of this "prima
donna," by no means "assoluta," at the court of a
very absolute King was not at all an agreeable
one; and she had not occupied it many years
before she endeavoured to liberate herself from it
by every device in her power, including such dis-
obedience of orders as she hoped would entail her
prompt dismissal.

On one occasion, when the Cesarewich, afterwards Paul I., was at Berlin, and Madame Mara
was to take the principal part in an opera given
specially in his honour, she pretended to be ill, and
sent word to the theatre that she was unable
to appear. The King informed her on the morning

of the day fixed for the performance that she had
better get well, for that well or ill she would have to
sing : nevertheless, Madame Mara remained at home
and in bed. Two hours before the time fixed for the
commencement of the opera a carriage, escorted by
a few dragoons, stopped at her door; and an officer
entered her room to announce that he had orders
from His Majesty to bring her alive or dead to the
theatre.

"But you see I am in bed and cannot get up,"
remonstrated the vocalist.

"In that case I must take the bed too," was the
reply.

It was impossible not to obey. Bathed in tears,
she allowed herself to be taken to her dressing-room.
She put on her costume, but resolved at the same
time to sing in such a manner that the King should
repent of his violence. She conformed to her determination throughout the first act, but it then
occurred to her that the Russian Grand Duke would
carry away a most unworthy opinion of her talent.
She quite changed her tactics, sang with all possible
brilliancy, and is reported in particular to have sustained a shake for such a length of time and with such
wonderful modulations of voice that His Imperial
Highness was enchanted, and applauded the singer
most vehemently.

When at last she visited Paris Madame Mara
was received with enthusiasm; and now was

formed the celebrated party of the Maratistes, to which was opposed the almost equally famous sect of the Todistes. Madame Todi was a Portuguese, and she and Madame Mara were contending rivals at the Concert Spirituel of Paris in 1782. These rivalries between singers have occasioned in various countries and at various times a good many foolish verses and *mots*. The Mara and Todi disputes, however, inspired one really good stanza, which is as follows :—

Todi par sa voix touchante,
De doux pleurs mouille mes yeux ;
Mara plus vive, plus brilliante,
M'étonne, me transporte aux cieux.
L'une ravit et l'autre enchante,
Mais celle qui plait le mieux
Est toujours celle qui chante.

CHAPTER VII.

CATALANI.

ANGELICA CATALANI was born in 1780, at Sinigaglia, in the Roman States, and educated at the Convent of Gubio, which she quitted at the age of 14; not before her wonderful powers of voice had excited so much envy and jealousy among the sisterhood, in spite of their renunciation of all worldly passions, that she was prohibited from singing in the church.

She soon appeared on the operatic stage, and sang successfully at Venice, Milan, Florence, and Rome. Her principal instructor was Marchesi; and in 1798, at Leghorn, she was singing with Crivelli, Marchesi, and Mrs. Billington. She was now invited to Lisbon, where she remained four years, with a salary of 24,000 crusados (£3,000). Proceeding thence to Madrid, she was flatteringly received by the Queen, and realized above three thousand guineas at one concert in that city.

It was during her stay in the Peninsula that she

married M. de Valabrèque, who was attached to the army of General Junot. Madame Catalani next paid a visit to England in 1806, and made a brilliant *début* in the opera of *Semiramide*, composed for her— in the days before Rossini—by Portagallo, whose music had been first introduced by Mrs. Billington in 1803. After astonishing all hearers by the grandeur and power of her voice in serious opera, she equally fascinated them the following year by her inimitable performance of the leading comic part in Mayer's *Fanatico per la Musica*, which Mrs. Billington had previously played with brilliant success.

In 1809 Madame Catalani gave a series of concerts, having seceded from the London Opera to which, however, she returned in March, 1810. She sang also at the Lent Oratorios and at the Concerts of "Antient Music."

These engagements she retained, with a slight interruption, until 1814, in which year Piccinni's *La Buona Figliola* was revived, after a lapse of nearly forty years, for her benefit; "when," says a contemporary writer, "an unbounded tribute was paid to her private character in her personation of the heroine, the 'Pamela' of the opera stage."

Paisiello's *Elfrida*, Martini's *Enrico IV.*, and Paer's *Camilla* were also brought forward; and, for the benefit of the Scottish Hospital, Mozart's

Nozze di Figaro, on the 18th June, 1812, in which Catalani was supported by Mrs. Dickens, Tramezzani, Naldi, etc. Some other of Mozart's operas were produced about this time, chiefly through the exertions of Madame Bertinotti, after whose departure the compositions of Pucitta, &c., were substituted, with little attraction but what they derived from the singing of Madame Catalani.

At length, after having visited the provinces, Scotland, and Ireland, and participated in the splendours of the season of 1814, Madame Catalani quitted England, where she is computed to have realized fifty thousand pounds, and made the tour of Europe, during which she was received with a marked respect probably never before experienced by a public singer.

From the King of Prussia she received a complimentary autograph letter, and the medal of the Academy. The Emperor of Austria presented her with a superb ornament, and the Magistracy of Vienna, to evince their sense of her benevolence towards their charitable institutions, struck a medal in her honour. At St. Petersburg, where she sang in the Exchange before an audience of about five thousand persons, she realized fifteen thousand guineas in four months, and received rich presents from the Emperor and Empress on her departure.

"These certainly," says one of Madame Catalani's earliest biographers, "are honours which elevate

the heart whilst they dignify the individual; and
that the effect of them should even afford some occasion for the charge of vanity on the score of
possessing such talents, and of the homage paid to
them, cannot be thought surprising; at the same
time that injudicious friends will, perhaps, be found
to put forth claims that provoke contradiction.

"At Paris, her management of the Italian
Theatre does not appear to have been satisfactory
either to herself or to the inhabitants of that gay city.
High in her estimation of the value of her services,
Madame Catalani has unquestionably shown the
most liberal feelings on many occasions in the
returns she has made both to charities and professors, as in the instance of Mr. Loder's concert
at Bath. In 1821, this extraordinary singer re-
visited England, and immediately gave a concert at
the Argyle Rooms, on the 16th July, which was
splendidly patronized, five members of the Royal
family being present.

"In 1822 she undertook a series of concerts, which
were attended by upwards of 1,000 persons, the
orchestra itself being crowded with auditors. In
these she aimed at a greater variety of style than
before, and introduced a song of splendid power,
'Della superba Roma,' by the Marquess Sampieri,
which electrified the audience. She also executed
the opening piece of the *Messiah*, 'Comfort ye,'
&c., in a manner, it must be allowed, more chaste

and subdued than could have been expected from her confirmed habits in a widely different branch of the art. She had, however, previously sung it at the Ancient Concerts in March, 1813.

" After this she again returned to the Continent, and was present at Verona during the Congress of 1823 as a private individual. Being subsequently engaged at two of the great English Festivals, she spent some of the intermediate time in another visit to Dublin, and after their termination made an extensive musical tour to Scotland and the north of England, since which she has again appeared on the Opera stage, probably for the last time, and given a series of ' Concerts Spirituels ' in London."

The anonymous writer from whom I have just been quoting bears testimony to " the purity of Madame Catalani's private conduct, amid scenes and temptations where numbers would have made shipwreck of all but professional fame ; and this duty," he adds, " is the more incumbent upon us, since in some recent biographies not only is the art of music treated as if it were the sole business of every man's life, but all considerations of moral worth are made of no account in comparison of the excitation of a sense of voluptuous enjoyment.

" Madame Catalani has a family consisting of two sons, the elder of whom was born just before her first visit to England, and a daughter, who is said to possess an hereditary talent for music.

" Endowed with the most extraordinary natural gifts, the image of resistless power and overwhelming magnificence, the first notes of Madame Catalani's voice can never be forgotten by those who have heard it burst upon the astonished ear. With this voice, extending in its most perfect state from G (below the soprano staff) to F in altissimo, full, rich, and grand in its quality beyond previous conception, capable of being attenuated or expanded into a volume of sound that pierced the loudest chorus, she bore down by force the barriers of criticism, and commanded the admiration of Europe. Nevertheless, it is, we think, incontestable that Madame Catalani is a singer of execution rather than expression ; indeed, it is scarcely possible that a person so peculiarly endowed should be otherwise. In the Italian, therefore, and not in sacred drama, must we look for her brightest triumphs. That her exuberance of florid ornament has not a little dazzled the judgment of the public and contributed to a declination from pure taste, we venture to express our belief, because it is impossible that so great an example should pr oduce a corresponding effect. On similar grounds we must protest against the transposition of tenor and bass songs to please the fancy of any singer whatever, merely because they happen to be standard works of art. We are compelled, likewise, to agree with those who feel that the human voice divine is degraded by singing passages written for the flute or violin, a perversion of the noblest ends of music which no talent can excuse, but which inferior imitators will, if not severely checked, soon push to an extent utterly subversive of all vocal excellence.

" Madame Catalani has never shown much predilection for the works of Mozart, neither has she until very recently selected many of Rossini's compositions for performance. But the subject is inexhaustible, and has perhaps been too long indulged in already. After all that reflection can suggest, or criticism descry, we are obliged to unite in confessing that there is but one Catalani, and to leave the final settlement of her claims to other pens, and to the calm judgment of a generation that shall survive to witness her successors."

In speaking of the singers with whom Madame Catalani may be classed, and from whom she must be distinguished, Lord Mount Edgcumbe writes —

" They may be divided into two classes, of which Madame Mara and Mrs. Billington form the first; and they were in most respects so similar that the same observations will apply equally to both. Both were excellent musicians, thoroughly skilled in their profession ; both had voices of uncommon sweetness and agility, particularly suited to the *bravura* style, and executed to perfection and with good taste everything they sung. But neither was an Italian, and consequently both were deficient in recitative;

neither had much feeling or theatrical talent, and they were absolutely null as actresses; therefore they were more calculated to give pleasure in the concert-room than on the stage.

" The other three, on the contrary, had great and distinguished dramatic talents, and seemed born for the theatrical profession. They were all likewise but indifferently skilled in music, supplying by genius what they wanted in science, and thereby producing the greatest and most striking effects on the stage. These are their points of resemblance. Their distinctive differences, I should say, were these : Grassini was all grace, Catalani all fire, Banti all feeling."

" It is well known," says Lord Mount Edgcumbe elsewhere, " that her voice is of a most uncommon quality, and capable of exertions almost supernatural. Her throat seems endued (as has been remarked by medical men) with a power of expression and muscular motion by no means usual; and when she throws out all her voice to the utmost it has a volume and strength that are quite surprising, while its agility in divisions, running up and down the scale in semi-tones, and its compass in jumping over two octaves at once are equally astonishing. It were to be wished she was less lavish in the display of these wonderful powers, and sought to please more than to surprise; but her taste is vicious, her excessive love of ornament spoiling every simple air, and her greatest delight (indeed, her chief merit) being in songs of a bold and spirited character, where much is left to her discretion (or indiscretion) without being confined by accompaniment, but in which she can indulge in *ad libitum* passages, with a luxuriance and redundancy no other singer ever possessed, ever practised, and which she carries to a fantastical excess. She is fond of singing variations on some well known simple air, and latterly has pushed this task to the very height of absurdity by singing, even without words, variations composed for the fiddle."

" Her voice," says Ferrari (Jaques Godefroi, a pupil of Paisiello), " was sonorous, powerful, and full of charm and suavity. This organ of so rare a beauty might be compared for splendour to the voice of Banti ; for expression, to that of Grassini ; for sweet energy, to that of Pasta, uniting the delicious flexibility of Sontag to the three registers of Malibran. Madame Catalani had formed her style on that of Pacchierotti, Marchesi, Crescentini [all three sopranists]; her groups, roulades, triplets, and *mordenti* were of admirable perfection ; her well articulated execution lost nothing of its purity in the most rapid and most difficult passages. She animated the singers, the chorus, the orchestra even in the finales and concerted pieces. Her beautiful‚ notes rose above and dominated the *ensemble* of the voices and instruments ; nor could

Beethoven, Rossini, or any other musical Lucifer, have covered this divine voice with the tumult of an orchestra. Our *virtuosa* was not a profound musician ; but, guided by what she did know, and by her practised ear, she could learn in a moment the most complicated pieces."

"Her firm, strong, brilliant, voluminous voice was of a most agreeable *timbre*," says Castil Blaze ; " it was an admirable soprano of prodigious compass, from *la* to the upper *sol*, marvellous in point of agility, and producing a sensation difficult to describe. Madame Catalani's manner of singing left nothing to desire in the noble, broad, sustained style. Mesdames Grassini and Barilli surpassed her on this point, but with regard to difficulties of execution and *brio* Madame Catalani could ring out one of her favourite airs and exclaim, ' *Son Regina!* ' She was then without a rival. I never heard anything like it. She excelled in chromatic passages, ascending and descending, of extreme rapidity. Her execution, marvellous in audacity, made talents of the first order pale before it ; and instrumentalists no longer dared figure by her side. When Tulou, however, presented himself, his flute was applauded with enthusiasm even after Madame Catalani's voice. The experiment was a dangerous one, and the victory was only the more brilliant for the adventurous young artist. There was no end to the compliments addressed to him on his success."

When Catalani appeared at the King's Theatre in 1824 and sang in Mayer's *Fanatico per la Musica,* the frequenters of the opera, who remembered her performance in the same work eighteen years before, were surprised that so long an interval had produced so little change in the singer. The success of the first night was prodigious; but Mr. Ebers (in " Seven years of the King's Theatre ") tells us that " repetitions of this opera, again and again, diminished the audiences most perceptibly, though some new air was on each performance introduced to display the power of the Catalani. . . . In this opera the sweet and soothing voice of Caradori was an agreeable relief to the bewildering force of the great wonder."

In one season of four months in London Madame Catalani, by her system of concerts, gained upwards of ten thousand pounds; and she doubled that sum during a subsequent tour in the provinces, and in Ireland, and Scotland. She sang for the last time in public at Dublin, in 1828.

As to the sort of engagement she approved of, some notion may be formed from the following draft of a contract submitted by her to Mr. Ebers in 1826 :—

CONDITIONS BETWEEN MR. EBERS AND M. P. DE VALABRÈQUE.

1. Every box and every admission shall be considered as belonging to the management. The free admissions shall be given with paper orders, and differently shaped from the paid tickets. Their

number shall be limited. The Manager, as well as Madame Catalani, shall each have a box.

2. Madame Catalani shall choose and direct the operas in which
she is to sing; she shall likewise have the choice of the performers
in them ; she will have no orders to receive from anyone ; she will
find all her own dresses.

3. Madame Catalani shall have two benefits, to be divided with
the Manager. Madame Catalani's share shall be free; she will fix
her own days.

4. Madame Catalani and her husband shall have a right to
superintend the receipts.

5. Every six weeks Madame Catalani shall receive payment of
her share of the receipts, and of the subscriptions.

6. Madame Catalani shall sing at no other place but the King's
Theatre during the season. In the concerts or oratorios, where
she may sing, she will be entitled to no other share but that
specified as under.

7. During the season Madame Catalani shall be at liberty to go
to Bath, Oxford, or Cambridge.

8. Madame Catalani shall not sing oftener than her health will
allow her. She promises to advance to the utmost of her power
the good of the theatre. On his side Mr. Ebers engages to treat
Madame Catalani with every possible care.

9. This engagement and these conditions shall be binding for
this season, which will begin and end (and) shall continue during all
seasons that the theatre shall be under the management of Mr.
Ebers, unless Madame Catalani's health or the state of her voice
should not allow her to continue.

10. Madame Catalani, in return for the conditions above mentioned, shall receive the half-part of the amount of all the receipts
which shall be made in the course of the season, including the
subscription to the boxes, the amount of those sold separately,
the monies received at the doors of the theatre, and of the concert
room ; in short, the said half-part of the general receipts of the
theatre for the season.

11. It is well understood that Madame Catalani's share shall be
free from every kind of deduction, it being granted her in lieu of
salary. It is likewise well understood that every expense of the
theatre during the season shall be Mr. Ebers', such as the rent of
the theatre, the performers' salaries, the tradespeople's bills ; in

short, every possible expense ; and Madame Catalani shall be entirely exonerated from any one charge.

This engagement shall be translated into English, taking care that the conditions shall remain precisely as in the original, and shall be so worded as to stipulate that Madame Catalani, on receiving her share of the receipts of the theatre, shall in no ways whatever be considered as partner of the manager of the establishment.

12. The present engagement being made with the full approbation of both parties, Mr. Ebers and M. Valabrèque pledge their word of honour to fulfil it in every one of its parts.

The free admissions in the shape of " paper orders " are said to have been intended for persons who were expected, if not engaged, to applaud; and in Messrs. Novello's " History of Cheap Music " we read that it was at one time (apparently about 1837) seriously proposed to introduce the *claque* at our Opera-houses, by way of " educating the public," and in order to teach ignorant amateurs where the applause should come in. The idea that a piece can succeed by merit alone has in France long ceased to be entertained. It must, in the first place, be well written, well composed, well acted, well put on the stage. But it will have small chance of success unless the attention of the public be called to its strong points ; and this, as French managers hold, is best done through the employment of professional applauders. The arguments of the managers on the subject are specious, if not absolutely convincing. No piece, they say, is ever brought out and left to take its chance unassisted by support from the front of the house. A certain amount of encouragement

is furnished, as a matter of course, by the author's
friends. Actors, too, and especially actresses, have
often devoted supporters among the audience. But
this was not enough; and it occurred, something
like a century ago, first to one French manager,
then to another, until at last the idea became
general, that the applause so useful in determining
the favourable reception of a piece might as well, if
supplied at all, be supplied systematically. Instead,
therefore, of making a distribution of free admissions for one particular evening, in view of a special
representation, the custom was gradually introduced
of giving them away every night, on the understanding, not merely implied as between friends, but fully
expressed as between men of business, that the
recipients of the "orders" were to applaud, and
applaud vigorously. Something resembling the
modern French *claque* seems to have been known to
the ancient Romans; and it may be in allusion to
this that *claqueurs* are often spoken of as "les
Romains," though "Chevaliers du lustre" is at once
a more common and a more romantic name for
them. But, so far as France is concerned, the
claque is quite a modern institution. It has not yet,
perhaps, attained its full development. It has,
however, already become an intolerable nuisance
to that portion of the public which goes to the
theatre in order to enjoy the performance, and to

note in an independent manner its good and bad points.

The origin of the *claque* has been traced to the custom, comparatively recent in France, of publishing the names of the actors and actresses in the play-bill. Until nearly the end of the eighteenth century it was considered bad policy to do so; for if an audience could be attracted one night by a favourite performer it might equally, reasoned the managers, be kept away another night by unwilling-ness to see a performer not generally admired. At the Grand Opera matters were brought to a crisis by an assault which a disappointed amateur committed upon a ticket-dealer who had sold him a place for a representation in which an obnoxious vocalist named Ponthieu took part. " Did I know that they would let loose Ponthieu ? " cried the ticket-dealer, when the man whose musical feeling he had been the means of shocking ad-ministered to him a severe caning. It was, in-deed, impossible for outsiders to know beforehand who would act and sing; until at last, in answer to the general demand, though in opposition, as it was believed at the time, to their own interests, managers adopted the practice, not likely now to be departed from, of announcing plainly beforehand not only what piece would be played, but also who would play in it. Then it soon happened that each actor of importance aimed at securing for himself a particular following; and this seems first to have suggested to managers the advisability of doing for an entire piece what the performers proposed to do for those portions of it only in which they themselves were individually interested. The applause, as before said, was systematized; and that nothing might be left to chance *claqueurs* were required to attend rehearsals and take note of the passages which might appropriately be saluted with gentle indications of approval, with warm expressions of admiration, or with outbursts of uncontrollable enthusiasm.

We know from the Memoirs of Alexandre Dumas the elder, and also from those of Dr. Véron, writing in the character of " Un Bourgeois de Paris," that authors and composers have often been consulted by some experienced leader of *claqueurs* or *chef de claque* as to where they would like the applause to begin. According to many a *chef de claque*, the dramatist is not necessarily the best judge on this point. What he in his semi-poetic soul may fancy will prove very effective is likely enough, as the *chef de claque* could tell him beforehand, to fall flat; whilst, on the other hand, situations, speeches, and mere phrases on which the dramatist has not · counted at all are at once recognized by the *claque* leader as sure, with a little judicious emphasizing from the hands of trained applauders, to produce effect.

The amateur *claqueur* became gradually a *claqueur* by profession; for in his occupation, as in all others, it was found that full success could not be attained without constant application. The *claque* was organized, like an Embassy, with *attachés* who were paid, and *attachés* who were unpaid; and the leader of a *claque* expected his subordinates to take instructions from him beforehand, so that when the hour of battle arrived his signals might be thoroughly understood and duly acted upon. For many years past the various *chefs de claque* have assisted, book and pencil in hand, at all the final rehearsals of a new piece. But, as a general rule, it is not found necessary that the chief should on these occasions be attended by any members of his band. They assemble around him at the first representation, entering the theatre by a private door before the rest of the audience, and taking their seats in the middle of the pit immediately below the principal chandelier. If they have been well-drilled they understand every gesture addressed to them by their commander; and their emotion, whether comic or serious, and at the same time their applause is regulated strictly by his.

In England the *claque* has never been, and it may be hoped never will be, accepted as an established institution, though it can scarcely be said to have no existence among us. The discovery of an

organized *claque* would at any English theatre provoke a considerable amount of resentment on the
part of the audience. Applause, once recognized as
paid for, would provoke counter demonstrations,
and the object of the speculators in this new kind
of merchandise would be wholly defeated. Allow-
ances are made in England for the exaggerations of
friendship when a new piece, which to the ordinary
observer seems to possess but little merit, is ac-
claimed by a select body of partisans as a work of
genius; and it is nothing but natural that those who
enjoy the honour of being personally acquainted
with a popular actor or actress should sometimes
see more to applaud in his or her performance than
can be easily detected by a perfect stranger.

Free admissions, too, engender among persons of
grateful disposition a desire to help the manager
whom they have to thank for a gratuitous entertainment; though such is the perversity of human
nature that playgoers who habitually visit the
theatre without paying for their places are apt to
assume critical airs and to remain studiously cold in
presence of even the finest performances. All things
considered, an English manager would find it very
difficult to secure a favourable reception for a new
play by simply filling the house beforehand with
what is technically known as " paper." Chance
plaudits, moreover, would be worth very little to a
director. To possess real value as aids towards the

favourable reception of an unworthy piece they should be under control; and the open visible direction of applause—as, for instance, it is practised at Westminster—would never be tolerated at a theatre where English, not Latin, plays were performed. When, at Westminster, the phrase "Davus, non Œdipus sum," or the line "Homo sum, nihil humani a me alienum puto," is pronounced, two monitors in conspicuous positions wave their wands in token of applause; and applause does, indeed, follow. But if in like manner we were called upon to applaud at the Royal Italian Opera Rossini's "Una voce poco fa," or, at the Lyceum, Hamlet's "Oh! that this too, too solid flesh would melt!" the demand would be met by a refusal, and something more.

If the *claque* really dates from the days of Catalani, it must be remembered that not she herself but her husband was responsible for the innovation. Strange that in the interest of so great a singer, so petty a device should have been adopted!

CHAPTER VIII.

COLBRAN-ROSSINI.

MADEMOISELLE COLBRAN's position in the history of opera and of operatic singers is marked by her connection with so many of Rossini's works; in which, from the time of her making his acquaintance, in 1815, until he ceased to write for Italy, she filled almost invariably the leading female part.

She played a leading part, too, in Rossini's life; for towards the end of his Italian career she became his wife. The composer and his favourite prima donna were married in the spring of 1822 at Castelnuovo, near Bologna. She was born at Madrid in 1785, and she is said to have been a great beauty in the queenly style : dark hair, bright black eyes, imposing demeanour. When Rossini first met her at Naples, in 1815, she was already thirty, at which age most women from the South have already lost a portion of their charms. "But only women of the best organization," says one of Mdlle. Colbran's biographers, "succeed as great dramatic singers;

and Mdlle. Colbran seems to have preserved youth-fulness and beauty of voice, and doubtless, therefore, of person, until long afterwards."

Mdlle. Colbran made her first appearance at Paris, in 1801, having previously studied under Crescentini, one of the leading male sopranos of his time. She soon, however, left France for Italy, and gradually found her way to Naples, where Stendhal, who occupied at the time the post of Consul at Civita Vecchia, seems often to have heard her.

The author of *La Chartreuse de Parme* and of the treatise *De l'Amour*, tells us in the "Vie de Rossini" that Mdlle. Colbran's name was constantly mixed up with political questions, and that it was at one time quite a party-word among the Royalists at Naples. Those who admired the King made a point of applauding that singer. "How do you like Mdlle. Colbran?" said a gentleman from England, one night at the San Carlo Theatre, to a friend. "Like her? I am a Royalist," was the reply. Stendhal, who was a Republican, justifies all he says as to Mdlle. Colbran's talents having been regarded from a strictly political point of view by recording his non-admiration of her. The Abbé Carpani, from whom so much of Stendhal's biography of Rossini is borrowed, was, on the other hand, a Royalist; and steadfast to his principles, he allowed Mdlle. Colbran's singing to fill him with enthusiasm. According to Stendhal,

Mdlle. Colbran's voice "began to deteriorate about the year 1816 "—the year after Rossini's arrival at Naples. But if such had really been the case it is scarcely probable that Rossini would have written for her no less than ten parts, including those of "Desdemona" and "Semiramide." It was probably not as a Royalist, but as a man and a musician, that Rossini felt so much attracted towards Mdlle. Colbran.

Rossini's politics were never, indeed, like the well-known politics of Verdi, of a pronounced character. One cannot imagine him in the character of a Revolutionist. But there is no reason for believing that, unlike other Italians, he took pleasure in seeing his country governed by foreigners, or by dynasties habitually dependent on foreigners for support. It may have been only to show that he was capable of setting to music no matter what words that he composed, as he is alleged to have done, first a hymn in praise of Italian liberty and immediately afterwards an anthem in honour of Austrian rule. It is certain that, when in 1815 he was about to leave Bologna in order to enter upon his duties as musical director of the San Carlo Theatre at Naples, he was called upon by his fellow-townsmen to compose a patriotic hymn, and that he complied with their request. The Austrians were not at that time in possession ; but they were about to arrive. When at last they came, and order was fully established in the previously

disturbed city, it struck Rossini that he might have
some difficulty in getting a passport.

The Austrian Governor, like so many of his fellow-
countrymen, was an enthusiastic lover of music,
and it occurred to Rossini that to ingratiate himself
with this powerful *dilettante* it would be a good idea
to present him with a piece of music. Accordingly,
to some verses in praise of settled government and
of Austrian beneficence, he set the music of his
Italian patriotic hymn, which since its composition
had been sung by excited crowds day and night
and was known to everyone in Bologna except the
newly-arrived Governor, his officers, and his troops.
The Governor, already prepossessed in favour of
Rossini and gratified at being waited upon by
Rossini in person, was enchanted when he saw what
the great man had brought him. He looked at
the music, saw that it was good, thanked the
composer warmly, and hastened to give him his
passport.

The next thing to do was to have Rossini's new
anthem played by one of the military bands; and the
combination of words written in one sense and
music composed in another is said to have been
irresistibly droll. Meanwhile Rossini had left
Bologna on his way to Naples. I may here mention that, without any perfidious intentions on the part
of the composers, national and patriotic anthems
have often by the force of circumstances been diverted

or perverted from their original meaning. " God
save the King " in its original Latin form—" Fac
salvum Dominum "—was, beyond doubt, sung for
the first time in the Chapel Royal by King James
II.'s choir, afterwards to be adopted with English
words—supposed, without much evidence, to be
work of Henry Carey—as the National Anthem, still,
it is true, of England, but of England ruled by
another dynasty. The hymn associated with the
Polish insurrection of 1863, " Boze cos Polski "
(introduced by Liszt in his " Polonia " Symphony),
was, as first written and composed, a hymn in praise
of Alexander I., viewed in his character of Polish
constitutional King, at a time when not only the
restoration of Poland, but its extension so as to
include the provinces detached by Russia at the par-
titions of the eighteenth century, was expected, or
at least hoped for, by ardent-minded Poles.

At a time when the Napoleonic kingdom of Italy
had just been broken up and given over either to the
Austrians or to Austrian influence, it was impossible
for any Italian to escape politics altogether; and in
changing the sky of Bologna for that of Naples,
Rossini found himself still surrounded by the same
political ideas. At Naples, if no feeling in favour of
Royalty as then established rendered Rossini an
admirer of Mdlle. Colbran, admiration for Mdlle.
Colbran compelled him to place himself, in musical
matters at least, on the Royalist side. Any dis-

comfiture of the National and Revolutionary party used, it is said, to be followed by special triumphs for the leading singer. When, on the other hand, the Royalists were prospering, their adversaries, unwilling to place themselves at the mercy of the police by hissing and creating a disturbance in the theatre, used to express their disapprobation of Mdlle. Colbran's singing by leaving the Opera-house in a body.

The first of Rossini's operas in which Mdlle. Colbran appeared was the now forgotten *Elisabetta Regina d'Inghilterra*. The honour of England was concerned in this work, which besides being borrowed from "Kenilworth," owed its libretto to a gentleman named Smith. Signor Smith, however, was no dramatist; and, instead of working direct from the novel, he was obliged to go for his plot and scenic arrangements to a French melodrama based on Sir Walter Scott's admirable romance. Signor Smith appears to have seen no beauty in the name of "Amy Robsart," for which — here, again, following the French play — he substituted that of "Matilda." Mdlle. Colbran in the part of "Elizabeth" fulfilled all the expectations that the composer, in his at once musical and amorous enthusiasm, had formed of her. An English connoisseur resident at Naples (possibly Signor Smith himself, though history is silent on the point) had undertaken to procure for Mdlle. Colbran correct designs from England for Queen Elizabeth's different costumes. Whether Mdlle. Colbran, the better to look the character, concealed her beautiful black hair beneath a fair wig is not mentioned in the annals of the time. But her success both as an actress and a singer has been fully recorded.

Associated with her in the cast were two of the greatest tenors of the day—Garcia and Nozzare. It is perhaps in consequence of the strange distribution of parts that *Elisabetta* has scarcely ever been played out of Italy—nor much in Italy, outside Naples. The parts of "Leicester" and "Norfolk" are both given to tenors; though if Rossini had been able to choose his own singers instead of having to accept those the manager, Barbaja, happened to have engaged, he would probably have assigned the part of the wicked "Norfolk" to a baritone. The character of "Leicester," an interesting lover, renders his position as tenor quite unassailable. But the rules of the Ars Operatica, as established in the present day, had not in 1816 acquired the force of law; and, as a matter of fact, there was no bass singer at the San Carlo Theatre (the baritone voice was not at that time recognized) capable of taking principal parts. It was still a conventional operatic rule that, at least in serious works, the leading male personages should be represented by tenors; the bass being systematically kept in the background, with no other duty than that of supporting the principal voices in concerted pieces. It was Rossini who brought forward the bass voice, and for the first time in Italy wrote for it parts in which independent airs were included. Basses were afterwards divided into ordinary basses—who still, musically as well as dramatically, were kept in the background—and bassi cantanti, who, like " Assur " in *Semiramide,* sang important solo parts. The bass was already in the days of Rossini's youth allowed to sing leading parts in comic operas; but in serious operas, and even operas of a serio-comic character, it was quite a novelty to see the bass coming forward as a leading personage with fully-developed airs to sing. Rossini at San Carlo had at his disposal no less than three tenors of the highest reputation—the before-mentioned Garcia and Nozzare, for whom parts were found in *Elisabetta,* and the equally celebrated Davide.

Although Rossini showed himself in Italy a most intelligent innovator, it must be remembered that it was not to him, but to Mozart and the other composers (for the most part Italian) who worked for the Italian operas in Vienna and Prague, that the reforms and developments afterwards adopted by Rossini were originally due. In *Elisabetta* Rossini may be said to have made his *début* at Naples quite as much as Mdlle. Colbran ; for until this work was produced the Neapolitans had not heard one note of his music. The story of his success in Northern

Italy, and chiefly at Venice, where *Tancredi* had been produced in 1813 with the most brilliant success, had reached Naples. But the Italians of the South were not accustomed to accept verdicts pronounced by the Italians of the North; and the composer, with whose merits the Venetians and Milanese were so much impressed, had yet to make himself known to the Neapolitans.

Rossini, when one of his operas failed, which happened now and then through the fault of the librettist, is known to have been in the habit of picking up the pieces and employing such of them as seemed most serviceable in a new work; and for the benefit of the Neapolitan audience he placed before the opera which he had composed expressly for them the overture to his *Aurelino in Palmyra*, which the year before had come to grief at Milan. The brilliant operatic symphony, which was afterwards to do duty, and which does duty to this day, as overture to the *Barber of Seville*, was much applauded; and when "Leicester" and his young wife sang the opening duet everyone was delighted. "The finale to the first act," says Stendhal, who describes the performance either from direct observation or at second-hand from the description given by Carpani, "raised the enthusiasm of the audience to the highest pitch; 'all the emotions of serious opera with no tedious intervals between,' such was the phrase of the general verdict expressed by the Neapolitan public."

At the end of the first act Rossini had made his mark; the opinion of Milan and of Venice was already confirmed by Naples. Mdlle. Colbran's scena was, however, in the second act; and it was not until her best opportunity arrived that she made her great success. Next came a scene for "Elizabeth" (in her correct costume as imported from London) and "Matilda," the substitute for "Amy Robsart;" and this was made the subject of a grand duet to which the before-mentioned scena leads up. Mdlle. Colbran obtained a further triumph in a brilliant show-piece which closes the opera, and in which Signor Smith, without the least regard for the great novelist from whom he had borrowed his principal scenes, makes "Queen Elizabeth" forgive the lovers and sanction their union. Mdlle. Colbran's final solo was apparently in anticipation, as regards form, of the famous "Non piu mesta;" not that this was the first nor even the second time that Rossini had brought the curtain down with a solo of display for the prima donna. Indeed, after the wonderfully successful rondo finale of *La Cenerentola*, he abandoned this means of effect, which was afterwards repeated by Bellini in *La Sonnambula*, by Donizetti in *Don Pasquale*, and by many other composers of less fame in operas of less note. The final air of *Elisabetta* had been so well designed for exhibiting Mdlle. Colbran's varied gifts and attainments that

Carpani summed it up as "a catalogue of the qualities of a fine voice." Some hypercritic ventured to object to the piece that it was not in harmony with the situation, which was pathetic, whereas there was no pathos in Mdlle. Colbran's solo. But though this was probably a just observation, the audience was so struck by the beauty of the music and the brilliancy of the singing that it applauded with enthusiasm, and did not know what a mistake it had made until it was enlightened on the point by the newspapers.

Rossini was unable to give a part to Mdlle. Colbran in either of his two next works, both written for Rome, where Mdlle. Colbran was not engaged. One of these was *Torvaldo e Dorliska*, produced at the Teatro Valle; the other the immortal *Barber of Seville*, brought out at the Argentina. In the former work the prima donna was Madame Sala, a very distinguished vocalist, who afterwards settled in England, and who, apart from her own career, will be remembered as the mother of our eminent author and journalist, Mr. George Augustus Sala. In the *Barber of Seville*, produced almost at the same time as *Torvaldo e Dorliska*, the principal female part was taken by the celebrated Madame Giorgi Righetti, though her celebrity seems to have been chiefly confined to the part of "Rosina" in the *Barber of Seville*, and of "Cenerentola" in the opera of that name. *La Cenerentola* was produced at the Teatro Valle nearly one year after the *Barber of Seville* was brought out; and owing, no doubt, to the influence of Mdlle. Colbran, consciously or unconsciously exercised, " Cenerentola " was the last of the great prima donna parts that Rossini composed for the contralto voice. He wrote no more for Madame Giorgi Righetti, but exclusively for Mdlle. Colbran, who was a mezzo-soprano. It was not until after *Semiramide*, when Mdlle. Colbran had retired, that Rossini composed parts for the soprano voice ("Mathilde" in *Guillaume Tell*, for instance); though the parts which he originally composed for the contralto voice (including in particular that of " Rosina " in the *Barber of Seville*) have for many years past been sung in altered keys by our principal soprano vocalists.

Rossini was still at Rome when the San Carlo perished by the fate reserved for all theatres, and which only one—the Paris Opera-house of the Rue Richelieu, which was demolished, stone by stone, after the assassination of the Duke de Berri on its threshold in 1826—has ever escaped. But Barbaja's fortune was not invested in one Opera-house alone. He had two theatres under his direction; and the principal one being burnt down, all he had to do was to carry on business exclusively at the minor establishment. Rossini had contracted to supply Barbaja with a new work for the winter season of 1816; and the singers of the late San

Carlo Theatre being at liberty as well as those of the still existing Teatro del Fondo, the company at his disposal was a very numerous one, and included more singers than he could possibly want. It is needless to say that the principal female part in the new work was assigned to Mdlle. Colbran, and there were two tenors to write for : not Nozzare and Garcia, as when Rossini was composing *Elisabetta,* but Nozzare and Davide. Rossini, too, with his ideas on the subject of the bass voice and the prominence due to it as to other voices, must have been delighted to find that Barbaja had among his singers a first-rate basso cantante. Probably it was at Rossini's own suggestion that this vocalist was engaged. It was for him, in any case, that he wrote the part of " Iago."

Nevertheless, it was for " Otello " and "Roderigo " that the best of the male voices were reserved. Davide and Nozzare were two of the most popular tenors of the day, and having them in the same opera Rossini was, of course, expected to turn this combination of talent to effective account. Mdlle. Colbran obtained a wonderful success in the part of " Desdemona." Rossini said many years afterwards, conversing with Ferdinand Hiller, that if any of his music survived him the *Barber of Seville,* the second act of *Guillaume Tell,* and the third act of *Otello* would probably live. The last scene of *Otello* is, indeed, as true an inspiration as any that com-

poser was ever visited with ; and those who forget
everything else in the opera will, once having heard
it, remember for ever the touching effect of the
gondolier singing the famous words on the subject
of past happiness and present sorrow, so applicable
to the case of the distracted "Desdemona; " and
the pathetic melody of the willow song, which, by
its simple beauty, went to the heart of Mendelssohn,
not generally an admirer of Italian music. Perhaps,
however, the music of " Desdemona's " willow song,
as treated by Rossini, is not specifically Italian. It
is appropriate to the situation, and might in its
essence have been composed by Schubert.

Mdlle. Colbran, by her singing of this song, moved
her audience to tears. Naturally she sang her part
throughout as Rossini had written it. It is sad,
however, to think that, when soon after its production at Naples the work was carried to Venice, the
" Desdemona " of the cast, equally with Davide in
the part of " Otello," ignored in the most shameful
manner the intentions of author and composer.
Davide seems to have been the person really in fault;
and, considering that the final duet of *Otello* did
not sufficiently show off his voice, he substituted
for it a duet of quite a different character from
Armida. "As it was impossible," writes a French
critic, M. Edouard Bertin, in a letter from Venice,
dated 1823, "to kill ' Desdemona ' to such a tune,
the ' Moor,' after giving way to the most violent

jealousy, sheathes his dagger and begins in the most
tender and graceful manner his duet with 'Desdemona,' at the conclusion of which he takes her
politely by the hand and retires amidst the applause
and bravos of the public, who seem to think it quite
natural that the piece should finish in this manner,
or rather that it should not finish at all, for after
this beautiful *dénouement* the action is about as far
advanced as it was in the first scene. We do not
in France carry our love of music so far as to
tolerate such absurdities as these, and perhaps we
are right."

Apart from the truly dramatic character of the
last act, *Otello* was in all respects a more dramatic
opera than those by the same master (or, indeed,
by any Italian master) which had preceded it. The
chorus in *Otello* is of great importance; and in the
finale of the first act the successive entry of two
choruses, each with a fine crescendo effect, is one of
the most striking features of this effective musical
situation. Every scene in this work is, moreover,
treated as a continuous piece of music; which was
a novelty in Rossini's time, although Wagner was
afterwards to treat as continuous pieces of music
entire acts. In Italy, moreover, it was something
new to hear recitative no longer accompanied by the
pianoforte, or by the pianoforte in combination with
the double-bass, but by the entire orchestra.

All Rossini's innovations were, as before remarked,

borrowed from Germany, or, to be precise, from the
scores of Mozart, which Rossini knew well. In the
present day every possible instrument is employed
in the orchestra. But in Rossini's time wind instruments, used sparingly in the orchestras of Germany
and France, were in Italy not tolerated; even
clarinets were scarcely permitted, and the orchestras of the Italian composers, before Rossini, consisted only of violins, or of violins, hautboys, and
bassoons. Little by little flutes and clarinets were
introduced; and in *Semiramide* Rossini gave great
importance to the horns—as everyone will remember who has once heard the famous overture to that
work. He had previously employed them in the
harmony, but in the overture of *Semiramide* the
four horns had a harmonized melody assigned to
them. Rossini's taste for the horn may perhaps
be accounted for by the fact that his father was a
professional horn player, and that he himself as
a youth was the same. " The art," says Fétis,
" of writing parts for the horn with the development of all its resources was quite a new one,
which Rossini in some sort created." There were
not only horns but trombones in the score of *Otello;*
all the brass instruments of the present day, in
fact, with the exception of the cornet, the ophi-
cleide, the euphonium, and the various members
of the saxhorn family, which were not invented
until some twenty-five years later. It was not

Rossini's fault that in his days they did not exist. He introduced cornets at the earliest opportunity in *Guillaume Tell.*

Mdlle. Colbran made her next appearance as "Armida," the opera with the duet which so pleased Davide that, as already mentioned, he could not refrain (in the absence of Rossini) from dragging it in at the end of *Otello.* As "Armida" Mdlle. Colbran does not seem to have made much impression. At all events the opera did not please, though it is said to have contained much beautiful music. The subject, for one thing, was somewhat old-fashioned. The singing of Mdlle. Colbran met, moreover, with a counter attraction in the ballet, which for the first and last time in an Italian opera Rossini here introduced. That he was a most brilliant writer of ballet music is well known to everyone who has heard *Guillaume Tell.* But in 1817 —to which year *Armida* belongs—it was not the custom in Italy to mix up dancing with singing. The operas of that day were divided into two long acts; and between these acts a separate ballet, lasting sometimes for nearly an hour, was performed. The long first acts of Rossini's operas are now invariably divided into two.

The ballet music of *Armida* was afterwards introduced into the French version of *Mosè in Egitto*, in which (produced in 1818 at Milan) Mdlle. Colbran created the principal female part. In her character

of mezzo-soprano she was beloved by Nozzare, the
tenor; and the two leading personages, in accordance with the device familiar to librettists and
dramatists generally, belonged to different and
contending nationalities. The parts of "Faraone"
and "Mosè" were both for the bass voice. Porto
is said to have rendered "Pharaoh" as important
a character as "Moses" himself; and it is recorded
of Benedetti, the impersonator of "Moses," that
he produced a great impression when he first entered, "made up" after Michael Angelo's celebrated
statue.

In *Mosè* the prima donna has not an exceptionally
brilliant part, though she has at least one beautiful
air. She joins, too, in the famous prayer, the
first of the kind ever heard on the operatic stage.
La Gazza Ladra contains a prayer in the form of a
trio, "O nume benefico;" and more than a quarter
of a century earlier Mozart had introduced a prayer
for three voices in *Don Giovanni*. But a choral
prayer was heard for the first time in *Mosè;* and
with its beautiful melody and its striking harmonic
change, it may well have produced a powerful
effect. The chorus begin the prayer; "Aaron"
continues it and is followed by the people. Then
"Elcia" repeats the supplication previously heard
from "Aaron," and the people again join in.
Finally the expectant Israelites fall on their
knees, and the prayer, with the key changed from

the minor to the major, is uttered by the solo vocalists and the chorus together. In " Elcia's " solo Mdlle. Colbran sang with particular charm and with the deepest expression. " It is impossible," writes Stendhal, who was present at the first performance of *Mosè* either in his own person or in that of the Abbe Carpani, whom he so often doubles, "to imagine the thunders of applause that resounded through the house. One would have thought it was coming down. The spectators in the boxes standing up and leaning over to applaud, called out at the top of their voices : ' Bello, bello ! o che bello ! ' I never saw so much enthusiasm nor such a complete success. . . . After that deny that music has a direct physical effect upon the nerves. I am almost in tears when I think of this prayer."

It may well be said that after the success of the prayer in *Mosè*, to which Mdlle. Colbran, by her expressive singing of one of the solo verses, had fairly contributed, Rossini became a firm believer in the efficacy of operatic prayer. Accordingly, in each of the four works which he wrote for the Grand Opera of Paris he introduced a prayer for the chorus; and never did his prayer fail in its effect. Auber, in *Masaniello*, profited by this new means of success. So did Donizetti in *La Favorita ;* while Meyerbeer was so pleased with the idea, or rather so pleased with its effectiveness, that he turned it to account in all his works :

in *Robert le Diable, Les Huguenots, Le Prophète, L'Africaine, L'Etoile du Nord,* and *Dinorah.* It is true that in *L'Etoile du Nord* the indispensable prayer is sung, not by the chorus, but by the prima donna with choral accompaniment. On the other hand *L'Africaine* contains not less than three prayers, all choral. There is a prayer from the members of the Inquisition in one act; from the sailors on board Vasco di Gama's ship in another; from the priests of Madagascar in a third. So great was the success of *Mosè* that it overshadowed the opera which immediately followed it, though here again Mdlle. Colbran was the prima donna. Associated with her were Nozzare and Davide, the two illustrious tenors, and Benedetti, the now popular bass. *Ricciardo e Zoraide* was the name of the work, which does not seem ever to have been played outside Italy.

Mdlle. Colbran next appeared in *Ermione*, based on the *Andromaque* of Racine. The cast included not only Nozzare and Davide, but also the celebrated contralto Pisaroni, who was soon afterwards to create the part of "Malcolm Graham." Rossini had previously, in *La Gazza Ladra*, written for the contralto voice the charming part of "Pippo;" the first auxiliary part for the contralto which occurs in opera. The parts of "Pippo," of "Malcolm Graham" (or "Graeme," as the Italians prefer to write the name), and of "Arsace," in

Semiramide, are probably the three best parts ever
written for the contralto voice, apart from those of
" Rosina " and of " Cenerentola," which are prima
donna parts, composd before Rossini had made
Mdlle. Colbran's acquaintance, and before he had
adopted the distribution of parts which was afterwards to be systematically followed by other composers. In imitation of Rossini, Meyerbeer wrote
one admirable contralto part, that of " Urbain "
in *Les Huguenots;* and Donizetti two, those of
" Maffeo Orsini " in *Lucrezia Borgia,* and of
the Savoyard in *Linda di Chamouni.* Since *Linda
di Chamouni,* produced at Vienna in 1842, character parts for the contralto voice have ceased to
be written ; and there are only six of them in
the whole range of standard opera, out of which
three belong to Rossini.

It has been said that one of the most important
parts in *La Donna del Lago* was given to the celebrated Mdlle. Pisaroni. The leading character,
however, that of " Elena," was still for Mdlle. Colbran. The opera was in a grander style than any,
including even *Mosè,* that Rossini had yet produced.
In each succeeding work he introduced broader
effects and increased the importance both of the orchestra and of the chorus. Much as Rossini admired
his prima donna, he was not infatuated with her
to such an extent as to sacrifice on the altar of his
affection the art which he also loved. The part

of " Elena " is a very brilliant one, and Mdlle. Colbran sang it with striking success ; but she had to
contend with formidable rivalry on the part of the
choral and orchestral masses. In *La Donna del Lago*
Rossini introduced for the first time a military band
on the stage ; and in the grand concerted finale, together with the military band on the stage, figured
a chorus of Highland bards with harp accompaniments. The ordinary operatic orchestra, moreover, had been strengthened by additional brass
instruments.

This, the most elaborate, most amazing combination that Rossini had hitherto presented,
threatened at the first performance to imperil
the success of the whole work. Rossini looked
upon his new opera as a failure ; and, leaving
Mdlle. Colbran to do battle with the public on
her own account, started the same night for Milan,
amusing himself at every stopping place on his
journey by spreading the report that *La Donna
del Lago* had been a prodigious success. He had
scarcely arrived at Milan, travelling thither by
easy stages, when he received letters by post informing him that the work upon which he had
bestowed so much pains had at the second representation been received with tumultuous applause.
The public had been startled at the first performance by the trumpets of the military band ; and the
would-be persons of taste among the audience

resented the innovation, much as a young fanatic who wished at one time to have Rossini's blood, and pursued him night and day to kill him, had taken offence at the introduction of drums in the prelude of the overture to *La Gazza Ladra.* In Rossini's absence Barbaja had reduced the number of trumpets in the military band; and this concession may, in itself, have had a favourable effect. In the first act Mdlle. Colbran had a duet with Davide, which was received with wonderful enthusiasm. There was a chorus of female voices, too ; another novelty due to Rossini.

It may here be observed that Rossini in his various developments and innovations was influenced by the materials he had to deal with. At Rome, when composing the *Barber of Seville,* he could not reasonably have written a chorus for female voices, seeing that at the Argentina Theatre the chorus consisted of male voices alone. When he went to Paris he found at the Académie a finer orchestra and a finer chorus than he had ever before had at his disposal ; accordingly in *Guillaume Tell* he treated with particular care the choral and orchestral portions of the work. In connection with Mdlle. Colbran, particular mention must be made of the manager, Barbaja, who was a great friend of hers until 1815, when she made the acquaintance of Rossini at Naples. Not that this new friendship seems to have interfered with the old one. Mdlle.

Colbran continued to sing at San Carlo; afterwards, when San Carlo had been destroyed by fire, at the Fondo; and a few years later at Vienna, where the greatest impresario of his time directed an operatic establishment, while he was by correspondence and through agents managing two others; one at Naples, the other at Milan.

Mr. Benjamin Lumley was alternately manager of Her Majesty's Theatre in London, and of the Théâtre des Italiens in Paris. The late Mr. Augustus Harris was stage manager of our Royal Italian Opera, and impresario at the Imperial Opera of St. Petersburg. Mr. Mapleson directed Her Majesty's Theatre in London, and the Academy of Music (where he had formed an Italian Opera) in New York. Signor Lago has managed the Royal Italian Opera of London in the summer and the Imperial Opera of St. Petersburg in the winter. But Barbaja kept going his three Italian Operas all at once; and it was much more difficult in his time to get from Naples to Vienna, or even from Vienna to Milan, than it is now to reach St. Petersburg or New York from London. Apart from all question of travelling, a manager must possess the highest administrative ability to be able to direct three operatic enterprises in three different capitals at the same time.

Barbaja, when in 1821 he was directing three or four opera houses (including at times the Fondo of Naples), had secured for himself a monopoly of all the operatic talent that was to be found in Italy, whether belonging to composers, conductors, or singers. Rossini had signed a contract with Barbaja which bound him to supply two new operas annually; and he was also to rearrange the music of any old works the manager might wish to produce, whether at his principal theatre or at the second Neapolitan Opera House—the Teatro del Fondo. Rossini was to receive two hundred ducats (£40) a month, with a share in the profits of the gambling saloon attached to the San Carlo. It was as waiter at the ridotto of the San Carlo that the future prince of operatic managers made his *début* in life; and though he possessed a sort of practical taste in musical matters he did not know one note of music. Such, indeed, was his ignorance of everything belonging to the art to which he owed his fortune that on a certain occasion when one of his singers complained that the piano at which she had been singing was too high he not only promised to have it lowered before the next rehearsal but immediately after the vocalist's departure ordered the stage carpenters to shorten the piano's legs by an inch or two. This story is also told of Catalani's husband, M. Valabrèque; but in connection with him it can scarcely be true.

The anecdote was told me of Barbaja by an Italian singer who knew him well and had at one time been a member of his company. It has been said that

Barbaja had monopolized all the talent in Italy; and the artists, who were engaged on the understanding that they were to sing wherever he chose to send them, were so numerous, that many of them were scarcely known to him by sight. Sometimes, moreover, he forgot that he had engaged singers of a certain eminence whose names and faces were alike well-known to him. Thus, happening one day to meet in the streets of Milan a vocalist of some celebrity, he talked to him for a time, and at last, in the most good-natured manner, offered him an engagement. " I am already engaged," said the astonished vocalist, " and have been drawing my salary for the last three months." Barbaja uttered a cry of horror, and told him to go without delay to Donizetti, at that time his musical director, and ask for a part.

It was when Donizetti was either musical director or pianist at the Scala Theatre that Barbaja introduced to him suddenly a lady who had come to him with a letter of recommendation, and whose voice he wished to have tried. As she had brought no music with her, Donizetti asked her to sing a few passages in *solfeggio.* Barbaja listened with much attention, and mistaking " Do, re, mi," etc. for the words of some foreign language, exclaimed that it would be useless to sing in that tongue and that to his great regret he could not offer the lady an engagement at his theatre. Barbaja seems, nevertheless, to have been a judge of singing; appreciating it

by its general effect while unable to estimate its
value in detail. It is said that one night, for the
sake of a joke at Barbaja's expense, some visitors
to the Scala Theatre agreed at a particular moment
to hiss Rubini in one of his best parts. The jest
was not in the best taste; nor, whatever effect it
might have upon the susceptible manager, was it
calculated to please the famous (and, perhaps, equally
susceptible) artist. When the hissing began Barbaja,
perfectly aghast, looked from his box, shook his fists
at the seeming malcontents and, alike indignant and
enthusiastic, called out to the universally admired
tenor: " Bravo, Rubini! never mind those pigs. It
is I who pay you, and I am delighted with your
singing." When, indeed, his singers were genuinely
successful, Barbaja was ready to defend them
against every attack. One day when a leading
lady of the San Carlo company (probably Mdlle.
Colbran herself) arrived at the theatre in a Sedan
chair she complained that one of the carriers had
been very negligent, having allowed the chair to
"bump" several times on the ground. Barbaja
called up the porters to his private room, began
by giving each of them a box on the ears, and
then exclaimed : " Which of you two brutes was in
fault ? "

Barbaja was accused of having established, in
conjunction with Rossini and with the powerful aid
of Mdlle. Colbran, " a regular traffic in virtuosi

resembling in nearly every respect the now happily
abolished slave trade;" and a self-styled "maestro"
wrote a series of letters on the subject to an Italian
newspaper. In order to carry out his plan, it was
necessary, said the indignant "maestro," to extend
the limits of his theatrical dominion beyond Naples,
and embrace a wider sphere of action. "Accordingly
people beheld him with wonder assuming in succession the pompous title of impresario at Naples,
Rome, Venice, Milan, Vienna, Paris; other theatres
still awaiting his sovereign will and pleasure. In
each of these," continued the "maestro," "he has his
agents; creatures who faithfully play into his hands
and second his designing policy. The plan is to
engage singers, and then exchange them from place
to place, and pass them from hand to hand, according
as the exigencies or the caprice of the moment may
seem to warrant. For instance, at Paris you have a
good dancer, and at Naples a good singer; but the
want of the singer is suddenly felt, or supposed to
be felt, at Vienna, and *vice versâ* of the dancer.
Well, make an exchange; never mind the lady or
the gentleman's vociferous remonstrances, that it is
contrary to the terms of the contract; stick to your
argument that the management engaged him or her
for his general service, and that that management
extends from Paris to Vienna, and from Vienna to
Naples—stick to this, and pack the complainant off
with a silencing threat of a breach of contract on

his or her part, and the inevitable consequence of
the same. After all, there is nothing so very extraordinary in this kind of traffic; do we not see the
peasants of Italy exchanging a horse for a cow, a
sheep for a pig, a mule for an ass, and so on ?
However, were things limited to a mere exchange
it would not be so bad, but what shall we say of
bonâ fide bargains made of singers to brother
impresari ?

" For instance, it is a known fact that Barbaja
sold the celebrated tenor Rubini for a whole autumn
to Signor Cartoni, impresario of the theatre at
Genoa ; and it is within my personal knowledge that
only last year he disposed of a whole company for a
stipulated sum to the impresario at Milan, and that
the company so disposed of was obliged, in spite of
all its remonstrances, to perform a certain number
of nights at the Teatro del Rè in Milan, the same at
the Teatro Fenice at Venice, and for a few nights
also at Vicenza. I have likewise heard from persons
of the highest respectability that the tenor Donzelli,
now in Paris, was exchanged for the dancer Albert,
and that this gave rise to so serious a misunderstand-
ing between Rossini and Barbaja that the latter was
actually obliged to hurry off to Paris with the irritated maestro. We have been assured that, while
at Paris, he intrigued with the directors of the Académie Royale de Musique in order to get them to
accept his singer, Davide, in exchange for Paul, the

dancer, but without success, as these gentlemen's consciences were really startled at the proposal, not having yet learned the secret of this scandalous traffic. In a word, it is known that at this moment there exists a private contract between Barbaja and Rossini to engage all the artists of merit of every kind, that by means of such a monopoly they may lay under contribution all the theatrical directions of Europe, as well royal as noble, dictating their terms for artists in the same manner as they recently did for Donzelli in Paris."

Mdlle. Colbran, however, was not moved about from capital to capital until, in company with Rossini, and as Rossini's wife, she went from Naples to Vienna, from Vienna to Verona, from Verona to Paris, and from Paris to London.

Mdlle. Colbran remained at the San Carlo Theatre for six years after she had made the acquaintance of Rossini, who throughout that period was under engagement to Barbaja. He was only bound to supply Barbaja with two operas a year—a trifle for him; and he was at liberty to work on his own account as much as he liked for theatres not conducted by Barbaja. During his artistic association with Mdlle. Colbran and Barbaja, Rossini composed for Naples eight operas, with *Otello*, *Mosè*, *La Donna del Lago*, and *Maometto Secondo* among them. *Zelmira*, too, was written for Barbaja, and in this opera, as in all the operas composed by Rossini for the most famous of operatic directors, Mdlle. Colbran took the leading part. It has been seen that Barbaja did not exact from Rossini all the work he was entitled to; and this was probably due to the success of Rossini's operas being greater than the manager had anticipated when he bargained for a regular supply of two a year. During his long residence at Naples, Rossini gave operas to Milan, Rome, and Lisbon; and in composing the leading parts of such charming works as *La Cenerentola* and *La Gazza Ladra*, for other singers than Mdlle. Colbran, he was guilty of notable infidelity. But the fortunate vocalist who had such a composer as Rossini to furnish her with parts may well have contented herself with those of " Desdemona," " Elcia " (in *Mosè*), " Elena " (*La Donna del Lago*), " Zelmira," and finally " Semiramide;" all written expressly for her.

When *Semiramide* was brought out at Venice in 1823, Rossini and Madame Rossini—as Mdlle. Colbran had now become—had terminated their connection with Barbaja; and it was nearly at an end when *Zelmira*, the last opera Barbaja was to receive from Rossini, was produced first at Naples and afterwards at Vienna. Mdlle. Colbran seems never to have obtained a more brilliant success than in this forgotten opera of *Zelmira*, which, composed expressly for Vienna (the preliminary representation at Naples was only a trial performance), must surely have exhibited the best work Rossini was capable of. Yet, in spite of its production, with Mdlle. Colbran always in the principal part, first at Naples, immediately afterwards at Vienna, and a few years later at the Italian Opera of London, it seems soon to have been laid aside; and for very many years past it has been entirely lost sight of.

Bearing in mind the fact that *Zelmira*, though first performed at Naples, was composed for Vienna, we may say that the last work Rossini wrote for Naples was *Maometto Secondo*, which was afterwards to be produced at Paris under the title of *Le Siège de Corinthe*. In *Maometto Secondo* Mdlle. Colbran did not obtain any remarkable success. Nor was this her fault; for the work itself, in spite of many beauties and of many grand scenes, did not make a very favourable impression on the public.

In the middle of December, 1821, the opera of *Zelmira*, in which Mdlle. Colbran (in association with Mdlle. Cecconi, Davide, Nozzare, and Benedetti) took the principal part, was produced at Naples as a preparatory step to the run expected for it at Vienna; and a few days after the representation of *Zelmira* Rossini took a benefit, at which a cantata, composed by him specially for the occasion, was performed. This, curiously enough, was the only work Rossini wrote for Naples in which Mdlle. Colbran did not sing. She was otherwise engaged.

She had to start early the next morning for Belogna, where a ceremony, more interesting even than Rossini's farewell performance at Naples, required her presence. Rossini accompanied her, and the marriage took place in the Palace of Cardinal Opizzoni, Archbishop of Belogna, who performed the service. Rossini's father and mother were present, together with the two rival but friendly, and, indeed, inseparable tenors, Davide and Nozzare.

The bride had not amassed nearly as much as a prima donna of the first rank may, with a very little prudence, save in the present day. Stendhal, doubtless on the strength of Carpani (from whose work *Le Rossini-ane* Stendhal's *Vie de Rossini* is in a great part borrowed), tells us that Mdlle. Colbran, at the time of her marriage, had property which brought her in an income of eight hundred pounds a year. M. Azevedo reduces the lady's income to four hundred a year; Zanolini, vaguer but more poetic, informs us that she possessed " a delightful villa and revenues in Sicily."

Rossini, his wife, and the two tenors, making a sort of family party, started from Bologna for Vienna, where the composer and his bride were received with enthusiasm. Carpani, whom Stendhal was afterwards to press into his service (though to Stendhal alone is due the observations on art, literature, politics, and society of which his agree-

able volume is so full), supplied Rossini with the
words of an additional air for *Zelmira;* and, following Rossini to Vienna, he heard that work performed
there a great number of times. After making
himself thoroughly acquainted with the opera, he
wrote an elaborate notice of it, in which occurs the
best account that has been written of Mdlle. Colbran's performance, and of her general style.

" *Zelmira,*" he says, " is an opera in only two
acts, which last nearly four hours, and does not
appear long to anyone, not even to the musicians of
the orchestra, which is to say everything. In this
extraordinary opera there are not two bars which
can be said to be taken from any other work of
Rossini. Far from working his habitual mine, the
author exhibits a vein hitherto untouched. It contains enough to furnish, not one, but four operas.
In this work, Rossini, by the new riches which he
draws from his prodigious imagination, is no longer
the author of *Otello, Tancredi, Zoraide,* and all his
preceding works ; he is another composer : new,
agreeable, and fertile, as much as the first, but with
more command of himself, more pure, more masterly,
and, above all, more faithful to the interpretation of
the words. The forms of style employed in this
opera, according to circumstances, are so varied
that now we seem to hear Gluck, now Traetta, now
Sacchini, now Mozart, now Handel; for the gravity,
the learning, the naturalness, the suavity of their

conceptions live and blossom again in *Zelmira*. The transitions are learned, and inspired more by considerations of poetry and sense than by caprice and a mania for innovations. The vocal parts, always natural, never trivial, give expression to the words, without ceasing to be melodious. The great point is to preserve both. The instrumentation of Rossini is really incomparable by the vivacity and freedom of the manner, by the variety and justness of the colouring."

With regard to the singers, Carpani praises in particular Davide, Nozzare, and, above all, Madame Rossini-Colbran—as the prima donna now named herself. Davide he calls "the Moscheles, the Paganini of singing," adding that "like these two despots of their instruments, he manages as he wishes a voice which is not perfect, but of great extent," and that "what he obtains from it is astonishing." Nozzare had extraordinary power, and was "more a baritone than a tenor;" which explains his frequent appearance in operas side by side with Davide. These rivals were not, indeed, rivals in precisely the same department of their art. As to Madame Rossini-Colbran, "she has," says Carpani, "a very sweet, full, sonorous quality of voice, particularly in the middle and lower notes; a finished, pure, insinuating style. She has no outbursts, but a fine *portamento*, perfect intonation, and an accomplished method. The graces seem to have

sprinkled with nectar each of her syllables, her *fioriture*, her *volate*, her shakes. She sings with one
breath a series of semitones, extending to nearly
two octaves, in a clear, pearly manner, and she excels
in all the other arts of singing. Her acting is noble
and dignified, as becomes her imposing and majestic
beauty."

During Rossini's stay at Vienna—and he remained
there throughout the opera season—he paid a visit
to Beethoven, who had heard the *Barber of Seville*,
had been much pleased with it, and had thought
still better of it on examining the score. Rossini,
on his side, entertained the highest admiration for
Beethoven's works. He said to Ferdinand Hiller that
in Beethoven's sonatas there were enough melodies
of the finest type for any number of operas; and
according to M. Arzevedo it was in conformity with
Rossini's advice that Habeneck first produced
Beethoven's symphonies at the concerts of the
Conservatoire. Unhappily when Rossini visited
Beethoven he found him in broken health, and
tormented in more ways than one by his incurable
and now total deafness. But Madame Rossini-
Colbran does not seem to have accompanied her
husband to Beethoven's residence; and it is with
her history, and not that of her illustrious husband,
that we are occupied.

Doubtless, however, Rossini's newly-married wife
accompanied him to Verona, where he had been

invited by Prince Metternich to the Congress of 1823—an outcome of the greater Congress of 1815. With a jocosity only pardonable in a diplomatist, the Austrian Minister, who had made the acquaintance of Rossini and his wife at Vienna, declared that "the first object of the gathering being the reestablishment of general harmony, the presence of Rossini was indispensable." At Verona Rossini was introduced to Châteaubriand, with whom he had a long and interesting conversation; and his happiness, as he told Ferdinand Hiller, would have been complete but for a colossal statue placed just above the orchestra, which shook with each musical vibration, and threatened to fall and crush the conductor, even as the statue of Theagenes—crowned fourteen times at the Olympic games—fell upon and crushed an envious rival who had plucked by the beard the seemingly inanimate effigy.

Rossini's "colossal statue which shook with each musical vibration" was probably a figure of Peace; which diplomatists assembled in Congress can sometimes only secure by crushing many legitimate aspirations.

After Rossini had completed—abandoned, one should rather say—his musical career, he himself had a statue offered to him. The inhabitants of Pesaro, his native town, wished to erect it. But Rossini replied to their flattering proposal that they had better keep their money and allow him to come once a year to Pesaro and show himself for a certain number of hours in the market-place.

Rossini had now determined to go with his wife to France. But before doing so he had to fulfil an engagement with the director of the Fenice Theatre; and the Austrian and Russian Emperors, after leaving Verona, went to Venice, where they arrived just as Rossini and his wife were working at *Semiramide*. As the composer wrote the music of the principal part his wife learnt it and sang it to him. *Semiramide* was brought out on the 3rd of February, 1823, with Madame Rossini-Colbran as "Semiramide," Madame Mariani as "Arsace," Galli as "Assur," Mariani as "Oroe," and the Englishman Sinclair as "Idreno." No opera of Rossini is more melodious than *Semiramide*. It is admirably written for the voices, and it contains some fine effects of *ensemble*. The chorus, the military band on the stage, and the theatrical orchestra are heard in combination; and the elaborate concerted finale to the second act (first act in the original) is one of the finest, if not altogether the finest, that Rossini has composed. The work, however, seems to have been of too massive a character to please the Venetians; and the music had to contend against the deadening effect of a dull libretto.

Of Madame Mariani, the original "Arsace," Lord Mount Edgcumbe, in his "Reminiscences," gives us some account. "She was," he says, "Pisaroni's rival in voice, singing, and ugliness," adding that "in the first two qualities she was certainly her inferior, though in the last it was difficult to know to which the preference should be given." This is very severe upon Madame Mariani, for Pisaroni was truly hideous. I am speaking now on the authority, not of Lord Edgcumbe's written description, but on that of a portrait of the lady, executed with scarcely a touch of caricature by Chalons. Madame Pisaroni was the successor of Mariani in the part of "Arsace," which was destined to be filled by a number of eminent contraltos, including Brambilla, Alboni, and in our own time Trebelli.

Among the most eminent "Semiramides" may be mentioned, in addition to Madame Rossini-Colbran, Pasta, Sontag, Giulia Grisi, Viardot Garcia, Sophie Cruvelli, Titiens, and Adelina Patti; though "Semiramide" will scarcely be numbered among Madame Patti's most successful parts. Madame Bosio, too, sang the music of "Semiramide" with great success at St. Petersburg in 1855. Malibran appeared sometimes as "Semiramide," sometimes as "Arsace;" and such was the extent of her voice and the versatility of her talent that she was equally successful in both these impersonations so different in character.

Rossini's reputation, as also that of his wife, must have been greatly increased by the visits to Vienna and Verona, where they made the acquaintance of many of the leading diplomatists of Europe, and were presented to several of the crowned heads.

The Rossinis were now invited by the manager of the King's Theatre, Mr. Ebers, to visit London. Not that the composer needed the admiration of the Sovereigns and Plenipotentiaries assembled at the Congress of Vienna to make him wished for in England; for we know on the authority of Lord Mount Edgcumbe that for many years after the first introduction of his works into this country " so entirely did he engross the stage that the operas of no other master were ever to be heard, with the exception only of those of Mozart—and of his only *Don Giovanni* and the *Marriage of Figaro.* Every other composer past and present was totally put aside, and these two alone named and thought of."

Madame Rossini-Colbran appeared in London as "Zelmira" in the newly-produced opera of that name. Unfortunately, the music, though much admired by good judges, did not please the general public. Madame Rossini-Colbran, however, appeared with success at a number of concerts, in which she was assisted by the principal singers at the King's Theatre, including Catalani and Pasta.

Rossini and his wife had come to London by way of Paris, where they remained a month. After arriving in London, they had only been a few minutes at their hotel when Count Lieven, Russian Ambassador, was announced. Rossini had made

the acquaintance of that busy female diplomatist
the Countess Lieven at Verona. She had spoken of
him to her husband, and the Count now called with
a message from the King to the effect that His
Majesty desired to see him before anyone else.
Rossini responded with a courtesy which some may
think exaggerated to this flattering invitation. He
had just made the acquaintance of the sea, and had
no reason to feel pleased with his first experience of
it. So upset was he that he found it impossible to
wait upon George IV. at once. He promised, however, to inform the King as soon as he got better;
and he added that meanwhile he should make a
point of receiving no visitors. He, in fact, denied
himself to everyone until, a few days afterwards, he
felt well enough to start with Count Lieven for
Brighton, the King's favourite watering-place, and
just then his headquarters.

Madame Rossini-Colbran made her first appearance in London at the first of two concerts organized
at Almack's for Rossini's benefit at two guineas a
ticket. The King had introduced him at the
Pavilion to many important personages; and the
effect of this attention was shown in the formation
of a committee of very distinguished lady-
patronesses. Madame Rossini-Colbran was assisted
by all the principal operatic singers in London, who
volunteered their services and would not hear of remuneration. The orchestra, chorus, and copyists

had alone to be paid, and the receipts were enormous. At the first concert a cantata which Rossini had composed for the occasion, and which was called "Homage to Byron," was performed. It was written for a single voice, chorus, and orchestra, and the solo part was taken, not by Madame Rossini-Colbran, but by Rossini himself.

Rossini afterwards told Ferdinand Hiller that he and his wife gained in London during four months more than he alone had gained in Italy during his whole career. Although singers in Italy were sufficiently well paid, such composers even as Rossini received for their operas the most miserable sums. "If the composers got fifty ducats," said Rossini, speaking on this subject to Ferdinand Hiller, "the singer received a thousand. Italian composers might formerly write heaven knows how many operas, and yet only be able to live miserably. Things hardly went otherwise with myself until I was engaged by Barbaja." Rossini went on to say that for *Tancredi*, the first of his operas which made a great success, he got only five hundred francs; and he added that when he received five thousand for *Semiramide*, he was looked upon, not by the impresario alone, but by the entire public, as a kind of pickpocket. Until he reached England he never gained sufficient by his art to be able to put by anything, though we have seen that Madame Rossini-Colbran, who must have owed so much of her success to the beautiful music given her to sing, had realized a considerable sum—enough to produce, according to one estimate, £400, according to another, £800 a year—up to the time of her becoming Rossini's wife.

Even in London Rossini did not make money as a composer, but as a singer, an accompanist, and as the husband of a prima donna. Still, it was as the first operatic composer of Europe that people in England wished to see him and to hear him sing.

" That," said Rossini, " is what my friends told me in order to bring me to it. It may have been prejudice, but I had a kind of repugnance to being paid for accompanying on the piano, and I never did so but in London. However, people wanted to see the tip of my nose and to hear my wife."

Having seriously gone in for money-making, Rossini and Madame Rossini-Colbran accepted engagements for private musical evenings, demanding for their services what Rossini himself called " the tolerably high price of £50." In the present day, putting Rossini out of the question, no prima donna of such merit and reputation as Madame Rossini-Colbran would sing at a private party for twice that sum. Probably not at all.

In London the Mdlle. Colbran of former days, the " creator" of the parts of " Desdemona," " Elcia,"

"Elena," "Zelmira," and "Semiramide," sang for the last time in public. After a four months' season she went with her husband to Paris, where he was engaged as director of the Italian Opera. The career of his wife was at an end, and his was approaching its close. He terminated it in 1829 with the production of his masterpiece, *Guillaume Tell*, in which there was not only no part for Mdlle. Colbran, but no part even for the mezzo-soprano voice. It was said that Rossini and his wife during their four months' stay in London realized no less than £7,000.

CHAPTER IX.

PASTA.

THE first great singer I ever heard was Madame
Pasta, when I was far too young to be impressed
by her; thirteen years later I heard her again, when
she was far too old to impress me. As to her performance in 1837, all I can remember is that, being
asked whether as a special treat I would rather hear
Pasta sing at one theatre, or see Tagloni dance at
another, I preferred the vocalist. She appeared at
Drury Lane, and, between two pieces, of which I
forget alike the names and the subjects, came in
front of the curtain and sang " Di tanti palpiti."
The simple five-note melody seemed to me then, as
it does now, singularly beautiful. I remember, too,
that Madame Pasta prolonged in a most remarkable
manner the shake which reintroduces the principal
phrase of the air. But the shake did not strike me
as beautiful in itself; and I had no means of knowing whether it was longer or shorter than such

things usually were. Everyone around me declared, however, that it was prodigiously long.

When I heard Madame Pasta a second time in 1850, I was capable (or, at least, thought so) of forming some opinion as to the beauty of her singing. But her voice was gone.

Madame Pasta may almost be said to have begun her career in London. She had for a few months played subordinate parts in Italy, when coming to Paris with her husband she made the acquaintance of Mr. Ayrton, who had just undertaken the management of the King's Theatre, and who was introduced to Madame Pasta at the house of Paer, the composer. Signor Pasta was an indifferent tenor; Madame Pasta a mezzo-soprano of promise. Mr. Ayrton engaged both of them for his next season; and as he had many celebrated singers in view who would require large salaries, he offered to the Pastas, who were obscure, small ones. The two together were to receive for the season £400.

Giuditta Pasta was at that time eighteen years of age; and, on the strength, apparently, of the name Giuditta, she is often said to have been a Jewess—as, without the slightest pretext, Rossini is set down by Hebraistic enthusiasm as a Jew. Her maiden name was Negri, and she received her first instruction in music from Lotte, organist at the Cathedral of Como, through whose recommendation she was admitted at the age of fifteen to the Conservatorio of Milan. After two years' study she left Milan and accepted the unimportant engagements already spoken of at secondary theatres in various Italian cities. Then, marrying Signor Pasta, she came to Paris in the company of the famous Catalani; and it was there, as we have already seen, that she made the acquaintance of Mr. Ayrton.

Signor Pasta, claiming to be a tenor, seems soon to have subsided to the position of prima donna's husband. He is, at least, not mentioned in the operatic annals of the time as taking part with his wife in any operatic performance.

Unlike Adelina Patti, Jenny Lind, and so many other famous singers, Madame Pasta did not come out in leading parts. Her engagement gave her £200 for the season, not £200 a night; and this implied modest impersonations. In London her first part was that of "Telemacco" in Cimarosa's now forgotten opera, *Penelope;* and she did not raise this inferior character to any position of importance.

Her next impersonation was a charming one, that of "Cherubino" in the *Marriage of Figaro;* and in this character she obtained marked success. Already she showed that her talent lay in simple but profound expression, not in florid ornamentation. She was emphatically what is, in the present day, called a "dramatic soprano;" though this did not prevent her from taking—like Madame Lucca in the present day—the page's part in *Le Nozze.*

In spite of her success as " Cherubino," Madame
Pasta did not on the whole make much impression
during her first season in London.   But several
critics had recognized in her the germs of a great
talent, which before long were to be fully developed.   Had Mr. Ayrton possessed the foresight
with which some of our operatic managers have been
blessed, he would have engaged Madame Pasta at a
rising salary for several years.   On the contrary, he
let her depart; and it was not until some years later
that she was to return to London, supported by a
great Italian reputation, and in a position, therefore, to demand her own terms.   Her first decided
" hit " was made at Venice in 1819; and her success
now went on increasing until she was engaged to sing
at Verona during the Congress of 1823.   Here she
was brought into personal relations with Rossini, in
many of whose operas she had already sung.   One
of her best parts in these days was that of "Romeo"
in Zingarelli's *Romeo e Giulietta.*   " Tancredi " was
another of her great impersonations; for at a
period when the male soprano was going out and
the tenor had scarcely yet come in, male parts—those,
that is to say, for lovers and heroes—were frequently
assigned to the contralto or mezzo-soprano voice.
Some years later the part of " Tancredi " was to
be sung and acted in admirable style by Johanna
Wagner, niece of the great composer; also that of
" Romeo—" not in Zingarelli's *Romeo e Giulietta,* but

in Bellini's *Montechi e Capuletti,* with a last act borrowed from Vaccai's *Giulietta e Romeo.*

All Madame Rossini-Colbran's characters suited Pasta to perfection ; and she appeared with equal success as " Desdemona " in Rossini's *Otello;* as " Elisabetta " in the same composer's *Elisabetta Regina d'Inghilterra;* as " Elcia" in his *Mosè en Egito;* and finally as " Semiramide."

In 1824 Pasta returned to the King's Theatre, where seven years before she had appeared with in-different success.   During the interval Rossini had, fortunately for her, produced several masterpieces, in which the principal female part was precisely suited to her.   When Pasta appeared at the King's Theatre in 1817, *Otello* had only just been produced, and had not yet had time to cross the Alps ; while *Semiramide* had no existence until 1823—the year before Pasta's return to the King's Theatre.

It was in the character of " Desdemona " that Madame Pasta renewed her acquaintance with the London public.   Determined, like all his pre-decessors and like all who have followed him as managers of Italian Opera, to bring himself to utter grief, Mr. Ayrton had engaged for the season of 1824, at a time when there was no opposition house to contend with, no less than six prime donne of the highest reputation—Mesdames Rossini-Colbran, Catalani, Ronzi di Begnis, Vestris, Caradori, and finally Pasta.   It was not until late in the sea-

son (as the season was at that time arranged) that
Madame Pasta arrived, and she made her reappearance April 24th. This time she had been preceded
by an immense reputation, and the house was
crowded to hear her. Her impersonation of "Desdemona" was a triumph of dramatic art, and her
singing surpassed all the expectations that had been
formed of it.

"Nothing could have been more free from trick
or affectation," writes Ebers, in his "Seven years of
the King's Theatre;" "there is no perceptible
effort to resemble the character she plays; on the
contrary, she comes upon the stage the character
itself transposed into the situation, excited by the
hopes and the fears, breathing the life and spirit, of
the being she represents."

In Zingarelli's *Romeo e Giulietta*, the lovers of
Verona were played by a couple of admirable
vocalists; Madame Ronzi di Begnis appearing as
"Giulietta" and Madame Pasta as "Romeo."

The last opera in which Madame Pasta appeared
during the season of 1824 was *Semiramide*, and in
this work she achieved her greatest success. A
good portion of this success must, however, be
attributed to the work itself, which was quite new
and composed in Rossini's most melodious and also,
in some scenes, most dramatic style. In spite of its
long succession of tuneful airs, now brilliant, now
expressive; its fine choruses; its effective military

music; and, above all, its magnificent concerted finale, modern opera goers, accustomed to more movement and less recitative, find *Semiramide* somewhat tedious. But the scene in the first act where the ghost of Nino appears, and the later one in which the Queen falls by the hand of her son Arsace, before Nino's tomb, were, in the year 1824, found strikingly dramatic. The witty, but sometimes over-ingenious Stendhal has, in his "Life of Rossini," made the unaccountable blunder of describing *Semiramide* as an opera in the German style.

"If Rossini goes on in this way," wrote Stendhal (in substance), "he will soon be more German than Beethoven." There are, indeed, some features in *Semiramide* for which Rossini was indebted to Mozart; and perhaps Stendhal saw Germanic tendencies in the prominence given to the bass character, who, in serious Italian opera (with the exception, indeed, of Rossini's own works), was not at that time in the habit of singing solos; in the great development of the concerted finale; in the character of the orchestration; and in the introduction of a military band on the stage. But is it quite certain that the presence of Don Giovanni's private orchestra on the stage, in Mozart's great masterpiece, suggested to Rossini the introduction on the stage of a full military band : a feature which was afterwards to be reproduced by all composers of grand opera, including, in parti-

cular, Meyerbeer? The whole melodic tissue of
Semiramide is, in any case, far from being German,
and thoroughly Italian.

After her immense success in *Semiramide* Pasta
found herself, so far as London was concerned, at
the summit of her fame; nor could her pecuniary
fortunes be carried much higher. She received for
her season at the King's Theatre £14,000, which
would be enormous even in the present day.

With so much talent engaged on such exorbitant
terms the failure of the manager was certain beforehand. At the end of the season not only were the
doors of the King's Theatre closed, but its contents
were offered for sale.

"Interminable disputes and litigations, mis-
managements and repeated losses," says Ebers,
" seemed to threaten ruin to whoever should be bold
enough to undertake it; but by some arrangement
the sale never took place, and the same manager
ventured to run the hazard of renewing his lease."

By one of those miracles of operatic management,
into whose mysteries the outside public are unable
to penetrate, the King's Theatre was reopened in
1825 with the usual flaming prospectus, and with a
fair subscription list. It was considered essential
to secure the services of Madame Pasta; who, however, was at this time singing at the Théâtre des
Italiens of Paris. She obtained leave of absence
until the 8th June, at which date she was to be again

in Paris. But when the difficulties on the French side had been surmounted there were new ones on the English side to deal with, and these for a time seemed insurmountable. The greater part of the magnificent salary promised to her for the previous season had not been paid ; and Benelli, the manager and sub-lessee, had left England. What Signor Pasta could have been about to allow his wife's affairs to fall into such confusion it is hard, indeed, to understand. Of his duties and responsibilities as a prima donna's husband he had evidently no conception.

Madame Pasta meanwhile, speaking for herself, declined to appear again on no matter what terms at a theatre where so large a sum was due to her for past services. " She required," says Mr. Ebers, " in addition to the remuneration which might be agreed upon for the employment of her services during the period of her *congé*, that she should be paid the whole portion of her last year's salary left owing by the late manager." An agent was despatched to Paris in the hope that he might be able to induce her to forego her demands on a manager who had disappeared in a state of insolvency ; and it was at last arranged in the interest of this defaulter's enterprising successor that Pasta should, without reference to her loss of the previous year, sing in London from the beginning of May until the beginning of June at a great reduction of terms. Instead of being paid at the rate of £14,000 for an entire season she was to receive £1,200 for one month's services. She appeared during that month ten times. But being free to sing at concerts, she accepted numerous engagements. She had, moreover, a benefit to take, which she sold to Mr. Ebers for £800; and in the course of one month she realized about £2,500.

She again made her first appearance as " Desdemona," and again so impressed the audience as to awaken, especially in the admirable last act, unbounded applause. But for Pasta, the season of 1825 must soon have ended with a general collapse; as from one cause and another Madame Ronzi di Begnis and Madame Vestris had left the theatre. Nor for some time was Madame Caradori able to appear.

At her benefit Madame Pasta appeared in Paisello's *Nina, Pazza per Amore;* an opera which, in the days before Rossini, enjoyed the greatest popularity, but which was now no longer to the public taste. She was more successful in the now equally forgotten work by Coccia on the favourite operatic subject of *Mary, Queen of Scots.* Madame Pasta is said to have impersonated the unfortunate heroine, " with an impassioned dignity and eloquence of voice, of look, and of action which defies description, and challenges the severest criticism. It was a piece of acting which great natural genius, extensive powers of observation, peculiar sensibility of feeling, and those requirements of art which are the results of sedulous study, combined to render perfect." The last scene, in which Mary bids farewell to her heart-broken attendants, is said to have been most affecting; and when Madame Pasta was recalled at the end of the performance she bore on her countenance traces of the emotion which she had undergone, and from which she had not yet recovered.

At the end of the London season Madame Pasta went in the month of August to Dublin, where her performances created the greatest enthusiasm. Her next engagement was at Trieste. After a tour in Italy, she reappeared in London for the season of 1828 in a new opera by Mayer, based on the Wars of the Roses. Madame Pasta wore the Lancaster rose, and as the "Earl of Derby" is said to have acted and sung in the most admirable manner. Then she undertook the part of "Armando the Crusader" in Meyerbeer's *Il Crociato in Egitto*, replacing Velluti, for whom the part had been composed. The male sopranists had disappeared, or were fast disappearing from the stage, Velluti being the last to go; and the parts written for this peculiar voice were now assigned to the mezzo-soprano or contralto.

When, at the end of the season of 1828, Madame Pasta took her benefit, she made a very hazardous experiment, which seems, however, to have been justified by success.

She appeared as "Othello" to the "Desdemona"

of Mdlle. Sontag. Here the music written for Davide, the tenor, had, of course, to be transposed; which alone must have been injurious to the part and to the opera generally. Pasta's acting is said to have been impressive and even terrifying; especially in the last scene, where " Othello " seizes " Desdemona" by the hair, drags her to the bed, and then, instead of smothering her, as in the play of Shakespeare, and in the opera of Boito and Verdi, stabs her with his dagger. Not only Pasta and Sontag, but also Malibran, sang this season at the King's Theatre, a combination which has never since been equalled; and the rivalry between the three distinguished artists is said to have been attended, at least in an artistic point of view, with the happiest results. Heartburnings it doubtless caused. But in endeavouring to outshine her rivals each prima donna surpassed herself. To Madame Pasta belongs the credit of having introduced genuine acting into opera. Before Pasta's time the Italian singers contented themselves with the conventional expression, the mechanical gesticulation by which operatic singing will be always more or less disfigured; so difficult is it to find vocal and histrionic talent combined in the same artist. But when Pasta had once shown how beautiful music might be rendered intensely dramatic the singers of her time were obliged, as best they could, to follow her example.

Malibran was in her way as great a genius as

Pasta; and in many of her parts Pasta was to be succeeded by Grisi, who, without being a perfect actress, possessed wonderful dramatic power.

In 1829 Madame Pasta sang with great success at Vienna; but perhaps the most brilliant of all her triumphs was achieved at Bologna, where, this same year, she sang successively in twelve of Rossini's operas, Rossini himself conducting the performances.

It was the good fortune of Pasta to be connected with each of the three eminent Italian composers who in the course of thirty years—from 1813, when Rossini produced *Tancredi* at Venice, to 1843, when Donizetti brought out *Maria di Rohan* at Vienna, and *Don Pasquale* at Paris—supplied all Europe with operatic music. Rossini had no sooner left Italy than his place was occupied by Bellini and Donizetti. The year 1829 saw the first performance of Rossini's *Guillaume Tell* at Paris, and of Bellini's *Straniera*, followed by his *Il Pirata* at Milan; and the year following, Rossini having now abandoned operatic composition for ever, Donizetti produced, also at Milan, his *Anna Bolena*. Donizetti had been composing opera after opera since the year 1818; but his works had made no great impression, partly, no doubt, because they were overshadowed by the superior genius of Rossini. In 1830, however, Donizetti was invited to compose a work specially for Milan; where, at this time, there was a remarkably fine company, including Pasta, Pisaroni, Rubini, Galli, Lablache, and Davide. The three leading parts in *Anna Bolena* were composed for Pasta, Rubini, and Galli, Galli undertaking the character of " Henry VIII.," afterwards assigned at our King's Theatre to Lablache, whose imper- sonation produced a powerful effect on all who witnessed it. Strangely enough, it was not until Rossini had ceased to write that Donizetti, in *Anna Bolena*, exhibited a style of his own. The dramatic character, however, by which much of the *Anna Bolena* music is marked, is certainly due to the fact that Donizetti was now writing for the most dramatic singer of her time. The first representa- tion of this work was given for the benefit of Pasta, who, in the character of the heroine, achieved a striking success. Rubini, too, caused much en- thusiasm in the tenor part, and especially in the scena with the melodious " Vivi tu "—more melodious, it must be admitted, than dramatic ; the second movement of the air being a little too sentimental and a little too trivial for a man about to die by the hand of the executioner. *Anna Bolena* was soon to be eclipsed by other works from the pen of the same composer, and it is now rarely, if ever, heard. Many years, indeed, have passed since it was last performed in London, with Mdlle. Titiens in the principal character. It contains a considerable number of expressive, singable melodies; and many of its scenes—especially the final one—are unquestionably dramatic. It may be said, indeed, to mark a step forward in the movement which has taken place from the style of Rossini, in his Italian operas (apart, that is to say, from *Guillaume Tell*), towards that of Verdi.

Lucrezia Borgia, produced at the Scala of Milan in 1834, was a distinct improvement on *Anna Bolena;* and this work, with *Lucia* and *La Favorite*, must be ranked among Donizetti's best compositions, though he was never so thoroughly in his own vein, and never, therefore, so entirely successful, as in his three comic operas : *L'Elisir d'Amore, La fille du Régiment* (originally produced at the Opera Comique of Paris), and *Don Pasquale*, written for and first performed at the Théâtre des Italiens of Paris. Let it here be remarked (though the observation has little, indeed, to do with the artistic career of Madame Pasta) that Donizetti's two great Paris successes, one in the comic, the other in the tragic style, were both to find their way before long to Italy, and to the cosmopolitan Italian operatic stage. Although originally composed for French audiences, both works are now looked upon as thoroughly Italian.

As "Anna Bolena," Pasta helped to secure for Donizetti his first great success. A year afterwards, when at the Cannobiana of Milan *La Sonnambula* was brought out, she rendered a like service to

Bellini; for though his *Straniera* had made a certain mark, and his *Pirata* a very considerable one, it was not until *La Sonnambula* was brought out with Pasta in the part of "Amina" that his name and his music became famous throughout Europe.

After producing in succession *La Straniera* (Milan, 1828) and *Zaira* (Parma, 1829), Bellini brought out at Venice his operatic version of *Romeo and Juliet* under the title of *I Capuletti ed I Montecchi;* which owed such success as it obtained to the singing of Madame Pasta. When we consider that Madame Pasta created in 1830 the part of "Anna Bolena," in 1831 that of "Amina," and in 1832 that of "Norma" (she had previously appeared with remarkable success in all the great prima donna parts of Rossini's operas), she seems to be the central figure in modern Italian opera: that particular school or style of dramatic music which, beginning with Rossini, has apparently come to an end with Verdi. The music of the Italian composers was for a time supreme in Europe. They have now to share the dominion with the composers of France and Germany; with Gounod, Ambroise Thomas, and Bizet; with Meyerbeer and Wagner.

The part of "Amina" in *La Sonnambula* does not, to the modern opera-goer, seem a very appropriate one for Pasta. It is a part which, in the present day, is undertaken exclusively by the "light soprano." One cannot fancy Titiens or Grisi in it; while, on the other hand, it was chosen successively by Adelina Patti, by Albani, and by Gerster (not to mention many other prime donne of less fame) for their first appearance in London. In Pasta's time, however, the distinction (due, I believe, to Meyerbeer) between " light soprano " and " dramatic soprano " had not yet been made. Every prima donna in those days was ready to sing expressive music or florid music : the music called " light," abounding in brilliant scale passages, staccato notes at the top of the voice, interminable shakes, etc.; and "dramatic " music, in which the composer has endeavoured, above all, to be forcible and expressive.

In *La Sonnambula* Pasta was again supported by Rubini, who shared with the prima donna the triumphs secured for both the principal singers by this melodious and truly emotional, if not conventionally dramatic, opera. The beauties of *La Sonnambula*, being of the simple and touching kind, can be appreciated by everyone; by the most learned musician and by the most ignorant amateur, provided only that the ignorant one has some natural feeling for music. Bellini had no warmer admirer than Cherubini, the composer of *Medea* and of *Les deux Journées;* and when asked, possibly by a pupil in his harmony class at the Paris Conservatoire, whether Bellini's orchestration was not very simple, and his accompaniments very meagre, the stern old master frankly replied :—" What other accompaniments could be written to melodies so beautiful in themselves ? " The success of *La Sonnambula* has been great everywhere, but in no country so great as in England, where it has been performed in English and Italian certainly more often than any other two, perhaps than any other three operas ; while no operatic airs ever attained greater popularity than the tenor air in *La Sonnambula*, " Tutto e sciolto," or the final rondo for the soprano, " Ah non giunge."

La Sonnambula had the incidental advantage at Milan of being well launched ; and it possessed the intrinsic advantage of being founded, with its thoroughly beautiful music, on a thoroughly interesting story, which had already been presented in two different dramatic forms before anyone seems to have been struck by its capability for operatic treatment. The French vaudeville of *La Somnambule* became, as rearranged by its author, Eugène Scribe, the ballet of the same name ; and this, in the hands of the Italian poet, Romani, became the libretto of Bellini's opera. To Scribe, then, belongs the merit of having invented the ingenious and charming story on which Romani's and Bellini's work is founded ; and the success of his simple, striking, dramatic theme shows, in a very interesting manner, that a story which is essentially dramatic can be successfully presented on the stage in any and every form, with

music, with spoken dialogue, or with nothing but
dumb action.

In 1832 Madame Pasta created at Milan the part
of " Norma," in a work which was received with even
more enthusiasm than *La Sonnambula*. In this opera
the tenor part, that of " Pollio," was undertaken, not
by Rubini, but by a tenor of the robust species, the
famous Donzelli. It is interesting, moreover, to
know that the part of " Adalgisa " was sung by
Giulia Grisi ; who soon afterwards was to distinguish
herself in London, not as " Adalgisa," but as
" Norma." The work, however, was introduced at
the King's Theatre by Madame Pasta. To judge
by the criticisms of the period, which were by no
means in harmony with the popular judgment,
neither *Norma* nor *La Sonnambula* could be looked
upon as great works, nor even as works likely for any
lengthened period to hold the attention of opera-
goers. Lord Mount Edgcumbe (who sets forth in
one portion of his " Reminiscences " that Rossini
was a tiresome composer, though he admits, and,
indeed, proclaims the fact that the public, having
once heard it, cared for the music of no one else)
tells us of Bellini's music, not that he did not like
it, for he had now ceased to attend the opera, but
that it was not to the taste of the public !

Stendhal, writing two or three years before the production of Bellini's *Pirata,* had foretold that Rossini
would be followed by a composer remarkable for the

simplicity of his style; just as it may now with
equal safety be predicted that after so much untune-
fulness the next successful composer in Europe will
be one abounding in rich melody. Bellini is said to
have had some difficulty in inducing Rubini to
abandon all at once his love of ornamentation; for
it was in the highly decorative style that this singer
had, prior to the advent of Bellini, gained his greatest
successes. Bellini passed much of his time with his
principal tenor while composing *Il Pirata, La Sonnambula,* and *I Puritani.* He sang the melodies
of his part as Bellini wrote them down; and the
composer at last prevailed upon him to deliver the
simple expressive phrases of his principal airs, not
only from the chest, but also from the heart.

Rubini, however, though I have been assured by
good judges that he sang emotional music in a manly,
vigorous style, must frequently have had recourse to
the falsetto voice; for which no modern composer
writes, and which modern audiences look upon,
with reason, as detestable. To hear a lover whine
about his love in effeminate tones is, indeed, revolting. The tenors of the present day sing the allegro of
the air, "Tuto e sciolto," in the key of B flat; and the
upper B flat is the highest note they have to reach.
In Bellini's manuscript, however, which, with many
other manuscripts, Signor Giulio Ricordi once kindly
allowed me to examine in his immense collection at
Milan, the air is written in E flat; so that at one

point the singer would have to strike the upper E flat—three semitones higher than any modern tenor aspires to rise; though Tamberlik, in Rossini's *Otello* (duet with "Iago"), used, in one of the most moving passages, to ring out from the chest a highly resonant C sharp. But E flat did not mark the utmost limit of Rubini's at once powerful and supple voice; for in the beautiful concerted piece which brings *I Puritani* to an end (and which, in a sense, brought Bellini's life to an end, since this was the last piece he wrote) he sang the higher F.

There is a legend on this subject, and certainly an authentic one, which was communicated to me by Mr. Mazzucato, son of the late eminent conductor of the Milan Conservatorio. Bellini was just finishing "Arturo's" part when Rubini, who was looking over his shoulder and singing the music as Bellini noted it down, mistook a D flat for an F natural, and, to the surprise of Bellini, gave forth the latter note. "If he can sing it, he may as well have it," said the composer to himself; and he altered the phrase in conformity with Rubini's new reading.

It is evident from what has just been set forth on the subject of Rubini's style and method of vocalization that tenor singing of fifty and sixty years ago, even after Bellini had done so much in the way of reforming it, differed for the worse from that of a later day. Mario had not nearly such a high voice as Rubini; but he must, at least in his maturity, have sung with truer dramatic expression than his voluble, yet, by all accounts, very forcible predecessor.

The style of Pasta, on the other hand, can scarcely have differed from that of the present day; or that, rather, which prevailed in the days of Grisi and of Titiens, for since Titiens' death we have had no prima donna who has been able to sing the great dramatic parts of Italian opera. Although Madame Pasta's greatest vocal successes were gained in the operas of Rossini, Donizetti, and Bellini, she was never more successful as an actress than in the now quite forgotten *Medea*—not the *Medea* of Cherubini, but of Mayer, under whom Donizetti studied. A story is told of a distinguished critic persuading himself that with such a power of portraying Medea's emotions Madame Pasta must possess Medea's features. Without some such natural conformity, he thought it impossible that she could at once by intuition enter profoundly and sympathetically into all Medea's inmost feelings. "Much," says a writer on this subject, "might be said in favour of the critic's theory; it is unnecessary to say a word in favour of the performance by which such a theory could be suggested." We are told that the believer in the personal resemblance of Pasta to Medea was, by way of a practical joke, sent a journey of seventy miles to see a portrait of Medea said to have been recovered from the ruins of Herculaneum.

" To rush off on such a journey with such an object," says the writer whom I have just cited, " may not have been very reasonable. To cause the journey to be undertaken was perfectly silly." As regards the music of *Medea*, it was found at the King's Theatre, as at the Théâtre des Italiens of Paris, that Mayer's simple and frequently insipid music was intolerable after the rich and brilliant compositions of Rossini. It was Pasta's delineation of "Medea's" thirst for vengeance and of her despair that alone made the representation successful.

Madame Pasta continued to sing, now in Italy, now in France, now in England, until the year 1839, when, coming back for the last time, or last time but one, to England, she appeared at the King's Theatre as "Medea," "Norma," and "Anna Bolena." It must have been in this year that I heard her ; or possibly she returned to London a year or two later. I, in any case, did not hear her at the King's Theatre, but at Drury Lane ; nor in any opera, but between the acts of a play ; or, more probably, between two separate pieces.

Unhappily, just as she was beginning to lose her voice Madame Pasta experienced a loss which, under the circumstances, was still more fatal. Her entire fortune disappeared in the ruins of a great banking establishment at Vienna. She now undertook tours in Germany and Russia which enabled her to save a little money for her old age.

" This famous ' cantatrice,' " wrote an eminent
musician who visited her soon after her retirement, " lives in a small house adjoining her own
villa, on the lake of Como. Close to the door
we stumbled on some prosaic matters—dirty
saucepans, kitchen utensils, and the like, not
to mention the leavings of an early dinner. Amid
this *débris* sat three unkempt girls, not one of them
in love with soap and water. At my bidding one of
them took in our cards, and the great lady soon
appeared. We did not see her at her best, for
having just risen from her siesta, in which we had
disturbed her, she was only half awake. We found
her very friendly and evidently gratified with our
visit. Her mouth and teeth are still lovely, the great
eyes full of fire, her black hair was in a dishevelled
state, and her dress an extremely original medley
of oddities. She never ceased talking of old
times, and told us she had given up living in the
villa because both her mother and her husband had
died there. She afterwards wrote something for our
albums, and gave us some beautiful flowers."

Moscheles said of Pasta in her best days that she
had a voice which " at first veiled, came out tri-
umphantly at a later stage, like the sun breaking
through the mist."

CHAPTER X.

IN France and England, but especially England, composers, singers, and operatic managers work habitually in hostile pairs. We have almost always had two Italian operas in London, though it has never been easy to make a single one pay. When Bach's music first came to England an attempt was made to crush it by means of Handel's; while the partisans of Bach felt in duty bound to retaliate—maintaining that, weighed by the side of the contriver of fugues, the great dramatic composer was of no moment whatever. Handel, again, by all accounts, thought very little of Gluck, and placed him, as regards knowledge of counterpoint, a little lower than his cook. Gluck, as everyone knows, was pitted at Paris against Piccinni, and it is equally notorious that Buononcini was forced at London into rivalry with Handel, to whom, according to some, he was "scarcely fit to hold a candle," though others held that Handel, compared to Buononcini, was "little better than a ninny." When Faustina was delighting half London by her singing the other half could see no merit in it whatever, and had ears only for Cuzzoni, whom the admirers of Faustina declared to be a most imperfect vocalist. At a later period all musical Paris was divided into two camps by the irreconcilable claims of Madame Mara and Mdlle. Todi, each of whom was put forward by her own particular set of devotees as the one great singer of the day.

Quarrels about singers assume generally a much more vivacious form than quarrels about composers; for in the one case the question turns upon principles of art, in the other to a great extent on personal charms. As Faustina to Cuzzoni, as Mara to Todi, so through the absurdity of operatic controversialists was Malibran opposed to Sontag. Sontag has been accused by hostile critics of singing too much in the style of an instrumentalist; though a perfect instrumentalist, like a perfect vocalist, must assuredly show feeling. Some ill-bred person is said on one occasion to have introduced to Mdlle. Sontag a skilful flute-player, and to have said to her after the flautist had performed some very elaborate variations : " Ecco il tuo rivale ! "

Sontag, in any case, moved the feelings of her audience; and still stronger was the effect she produced on the hearts of her private hearers. When she was singing at Berlin during the height of her success in the first period of her career, Lord Clanwilliam, the English Ambassador, became so much attached to her, and pursued her so persistently wherever she went that to indicate his habit of following " Sontag," people called him " Lord Montag." In obedience to the general law which seems to govern the fate of prime donne, Sontag married brilliantly; though it cannot be affirmed with any certainty that she married happily. A native of Coblenz, born in 1805, she appeared at an early age with the most decided success at Berlin, Vienna, Paris, and London. At Vienna, in 1823, she sang the principal part in Weber's beautiful opera of *Euryanthe*, which, by many of its melodic phrases, suggests the affinity that certainly exists between the genius of Weber and that of Wagner; and she soon afterwards appeared at the Théâtre des Italiens of Paris as " Rosina," in the *Barber of Seville*, this being the first occasion of her singing in the Italian language. On hearing her, Catalani is said to have made the ingenious but possibly not truthful remark : " Elle est la première dans son genre, mais son genre n'est pas le premier." Contemporary chroniclers record with admiration the fact that she received as salary £2,000 a year. A vocalist of first renown earns in the present day £20,000.

Henriette Sontag, to narrate her life in some detail, was the daughter of an actor, Franz Anton

Sontag, and an actress, Franziska Marklof, who, playing together in the same company, became attached to one another, and in 1805 got married. According to Karoline Bauer, who knew the famous singer well, and speaks of her frequently in her Memoirs, Henriette Sontag assumed as a matter of taste and fancy the Christian name by which she was to become generally known. She was born on the 3rd of January, 1806; and Karoline Bauer assures us that she was named in baptism Gertrudis Walpurgis. The little girl was taken by her mother to a fortune-teller, who prophesied that the child's fame would one day re-echo " over lands and seas." At the age of seven little Sontag played and sung the part of " Lilli " in *Donauweibchen.* Her next appearance was at Prague, where she sang two little airs in Wranitzky's *Oberon* so successfully that the director of the theatre, Liebic by name, placed her in the local Conservatoire, where she studied music and singing in a systematic manner.

In 1818, still a child, she sang the part of " Benjamin " in Méhul's *Joseph;* and two years later she gained a positive triumph as the Princess in Boieldieu's *Jean de Paris.* From Prague she passed to Vienna, where she was engaged for four years to sing both in German and Italian opera. What was called German Opera was often Italian or French Opera translated into German; and one of Henriette's best parts was that of the heroine in *La Dame*

Blanche. In the year 1826 Henriette Sontag was singing at Berlin; as to which the following entry may be cited from Moscheles' diary : " Concert day. Fräulein Sontag, who was not permitted to lend me her active aid because the managers of the Königstadt refused their permission to any singing of hers out of the theatre, assisted me passively by reporting herself hoarse instead of singing in *Sargin;* she came with my wife to my concert. When I thanked the celebrated singer she said with the sweet smile peculiar to her, 'But, dear Moscheles, should not an old Vienna friend help to frustrate the cabal of a theatrical manager ? ' Jettel is still Jettel."

Of the extent to which heads were turned by Henriette's beautiful singing, graceful person, and fascinating ways, I may here cite some passages from a little book published at Leipsic in 1826 by "Freimund Zuschauer," under the title of "Henrietta, the beautiful singer : a story of our days." The author thus describes one of Mdlle. Sontag's first appearances at the Königstadt Theatre, Berlin : " The opera was at an end; but the volleys of applause which were to do appreciative honour to the talents of the young singer, Henriette, who had just made her *début* as a newly-engaged member of the theatre, seemed to go on for ever. Ever anew the noisy clapping of thousands of eager hands was heard, mingled with the incessant call of the name

of the beautiful lady. At last the curtain rose
again. The lovely angel appeared in all the grace-
fulness with which she had charmed the audience the
whole evening. Compared with the noise that now
rang through the house, the previous clamour might
be called stillness. Everybody abandoned himself
to the loudest outbursts of transport. Only the
young songstress herself was not allowed to express
her feelings in words, and had to retire with silent
bows; but her eyes, sparkling with pleasure, plainly
betokened what she felt. However, almost plainer
still spoke the looks of all the gentlemen, both young
and old, in the theatre; none were there out of
whose eyes the god of love did not peep mockingly.
Even old Field Marshal von Ranwitz [General von
Brauchitsch, Commandant of Berlin]—upon whose
head, grown grey in wars, one could scarcely count
a single hair—even he, in his great age, seemed to
be struck by an arrow against which he probably
thought himself too securely armoured. Not
only had he tried to arm his breast with a hard
brazen armour against Cupid's shots, but his pre-
caution went further; for even his face, not excluding
the nose, he had, with the aid of Bacchus, who is a
better workman in copper than Vulcan, covered with
a purple coat of that glowing metal. His eyes, in
order to be safe there also, had the same kind god,
Bacchus, helped to turn into a glassy state. But
Cupid, defying the defensive alliance, had neverthe-

less penetrated, how, the gods alone know. He had certainly done so ; for the Adjutant heard the Marshal say on leaving his box, ' I would forego the aroma of Pontac for three days if thereby I could purchase one kiss from this wonderfully pretty girl;' and he could not have employed a stronger affirmation. Major Regelino [Zechelin] had suffered in a similar way, who although he had almost become a fixture at the Casino consented this once to miss his game and to dream in the Opera, for he had probably heard nothing, so much had the young singer blinded, nay, stunned him.   When he entered his carriage he called out to the coachman, ' To the Königstadt Theatre ! '—which he was just leaving.

" More than these two royal counsellors, ' Hemmstoff ' [Hermstorff] and ' Wicke ' [Wilke], intimate friends through similarity of artistic inclinations and theatrical habits, I say still more were these captivated by the wondrous phenomenon. Wicke allowed his languishing eye to linger once more upon the drawn curtain ; then he said, ' Friend, what is life without the delight of love ?   Oh, now do I understand the tender-hearted poet ! ' ' True, very true ! ' Hemmstoff replied, in vain trying to put his hand through his hair (for the scythe of time had moved from his head this stately ornament, and only from former habit made he this movement of negligent elegance) ; ' the poet's words are true, very true

indeed. Oh, I feel confoundedly hungry. Let us
eat something downstairs in the dining-rooms.'

"Now there below are found assembled the whole
of the old and young Sontag guards over oysters
and champagne, singing the praises of the beautiful
Henriette. A French Abbé, with a large pate still
balder than Hemmstoff's; a tall, thin man in a blue
dress-coat, wearing a cross in his button-hole, with
grey, carefully-dressed hair, red face, puckered into
a thousand folds, dressed like a dandy of twenty-
five. He was styled Lieutenant-Colonel [Von
Freskow]. Then came the young stage-manager of
the Königstadt Theatre, Karl von Holtei."

Among the critics assembled to hear the new
singer are Rellstab, described as "A stout youth,
with a moustache, and a big pair of spectacles, who
affects to be wise, and turns up his nose at everything," though, as Karoline Bauer remarks, he could
not turn up his nose very much, because it was too
flat; and Saphir, the Hebrew-German satirist, who,
after making Munich too hot to hold him, had taken
refuge at Vienna. Among the admirers of the lively
Henriette, pre-eminence is given to Lord Clanwilliam,
English Ambassador at Vienna, already referred to
as bearing the nickname of "Lord Montag." Two
of them are said to have distinguished themselves in
a duel, of which the last available ticket for one of
Sontag's performances was the cause. So when Le

Sage's "Diable Boiteux" was published, the last remaining copy of the first edition was fought for by two determined admirers of the author's genius.

Henriette was very much mortified by the jests of this not too-witty squib. At first Saphir was suspected of having written it; but he repudiated the idea, saying that if he had been the author, the pamphlet would have been better written, wittier, and more severe.

Saphir, however, had been making jokes at Mdlle. Sontag's expense in his journal; and in Varnhagen's diary the following entry appears:— " Mdlle. Sontag, the singer, has applied to the King, and requested him to protect her from the attacks which Herr Saphir is constantly making in his *Schnellpost.* The King issued a private order to his Minister, Schuckmann, and the latter a rescript to Saphir, in which he was forbidden all personal attacks, and more especially any directed against Mdlle. Sontag." Then it was said that Karl von Holtei was the author of the hateful pamphlet, he being the only man mentioned in it who was praised; and it was suggested that he wanted to avenge himself on Lord Clanwilliam; the rich English lord being so formidable a rival to the poor German poet. At last it was discovered that Rellstab, the musical critic, was the author of the offensive publication; and now the whole of Sontag's admirers, the so-called " Sontag-guards," were upon him. He received challenges without number. Lord Clanwilliam, at the suggestion of the Foreign Minister, brought an action against him; and Rellstab, found guilty in two instances of slander, was sentenced to three months' confinement in a fortress.

When, at the end of May, 1826, Sontag left Berlin, though only for a few months, her departure was the signal for a universal burst of enthusiasm and of grief, not to say despair. Mdlle. Sontag was about to fulfil an engagement of a few months only at Paris. Holtei on this occasion wrote no less than six sonnets on the subject of the loved-one's departure; and he fluttered them, printed on white satin, on to the stage. In a poem addressed to her by Friedrich Förster occurred these words of menace to the French :—" If you should try to keep this nightingale for Paris, then we must show you that we can again fetch back our Victoria from the Seine." This referred to a statue of the goddess of Victory which the French had seized during the wars and carried to Paris, whence it was brought back to Berlin by Blucher.

So many demonstrations of fervent admiration moved the departing singer to tears. She sobbed and exclaimed, " I do not deserve so much love and goodwill." Outside the theatre she had to say good-bye to thousands of admirers who had not been able to gain admission. They received her with enthusiastic cheers, and as she drove to her hotel she found the road strewn with flowers. Then the goddess, soon to be exiled, received in her apartments a select but still numerous body of admirers. Outside there was a torchlight procession, also a serenade performed by several military bands in combination. An enormous crowd applauded her from the street; and when from time to time she appeared at the balcony to wave her handkerchief, excited voices cried out, " Come back ! come back ! "

After Sontag had started, the very witty but still more malicious Saphir wrote in the *Schnellpost*, " that the singer, so much admired by the Berlinese, would make a terrible *fiasco* at Paris by the side of artists like Pasta and Malibran. This pretty little vocalist in the small Italian style," he continued, " wants deepfelt, tragic, and genuine passion to carry the French away with her." Her singing lacked the genuine Italian *portamento*, nor was even her figure perfect.

This time Saphir had only put forth a critical opinion, and the law could not touch him; but his article caused much ill-feeling, or rather it produced a just feeling of indignation.

It was at Munich, and above all at Vienna, that this amusing wit distinguished himself. He could neither rise to such heights nor penetrate to such depths as Heine: most witty of poets, most poetical of wits. But he had wit of a certain order constantly at his hand. At Munich he vexed the King to the heart by ridiculing His Majesty's bad verses. Once when a crowd had assembled before the Palace Saphir related in his journal (wherever he went he started a newspaper) how, a mob of malcontents having collected in front of the Palace, all the best known means of dispersing it were tried, but in vain. The people were threatened with the fire of infantry; cavalry prepared to charge them; pieces of artillery were pointed at them; but all without result. At last His Majesty appeared at the balcony and began to read one of his poems; upon which the vast concourse broke up and fled in every direction.

Unable to tolerate banter of this kind, the King sent a commissary of police to Herr Saphir with an order to leave within twenty-four hours. The commissary was a polite, considerate man; and he expressed a fear lest Herr Saphir should be unable to get away so quickly. "I think I can manage it," replied Saphir, "but if not, I will borrow some superfluous feet from His Majesty's verses." The demonstration in front of the palace had been provoked by a rise in the price of beer. Struck by the capacity of the Bavarians in the way of beer drinking, Saphir said of them that they were beer barrels in the morning and barrels of beer at night. A newly-married couple calling on him one day with a letter of introduction, he was struck by the effeminate appearance of the young husband, and before entering into conversation said, with a deferential air : " Allow me first to ask—which of you is the bride ? "

Having been rudely treated in a second-class railway carriage, he afterwards said in reference to the incident :—"In the first-class the passengers are rude to the guard ; in the third the guard is rude to the passengers ; in the second the passengers are rude to one another."

Of a dull place in the country, he remarked that, " If it were not for an occasional death there would be no life in it whatever."

With managers he was constantly getting into trouble ; and when the director of one of the Vienna theatres procured an order forbidding Saphir to enter his house, he remarked that he could not complain of being kept out of the theatre, but that it would have been cruel indeed had he been commanded, once inside, not to leave till the performance came to an end.

No wonder that when spiteful things were written about actresses and singers the first man they thought of as their possible enemy was Saphir. In spite of his prophecies (ridiculous in an artistic point of view, regard being paid to the grounds on which they were based), Sontag gained in Paris the most brilliant success; and by no one was she better received than by Pasta and Malibran.

Returning from Paris, Sontag was to receive a great honour and enjoy a great pleasure. She sang to Goethe, and what Goethe thought of her singing is set forth in the following letter addressed by him to Zelter on the 9th September, 1826. It is indeed a characteristic letter on the part of the old poet, critic, and philosopher, then in his seventy-eighth year.

" That Mdlle. Sontag has now also passed us, dispensing melody and music, makes at any rate an epoch. To be sure, everybody says that one ought to hear her often ; and hundreds would gladly sit again in the Königstadt Theatre to-day and all day, and I among them. For, properly speaking, one ought to conceive and comprehend her first as an individual, recognize her as an element of the time, assimilate one's self with her, accustom one's self to her ; then she must needs remain a sweet, agreeable enjoyment. But heard thus, *extempore*, her talent has more confused than comforted me. The good that passes by without returning leaves behind it an impression which may be compared to a vacuum ; it is felt like a want."

Mdlle. Sontag had become quite an historical personage. In Varnhagen's diary we find this second entry concerning her :—

" Mdlle. Sontag and Madame Lemière-Desarges

are daily in the society of Princess Liegnitz; the former instructs her in playing the pianoforte, the latter gives her lessons in dancing, French conversation, and various forms of deportment."

Rellstab, the critic, who had been imprisoned on account of the libellous matter contained in the Zuschauer pamphlet on the subject of the Sontag mania, affected, after his liberation, to bear no malice towards the singer who had been indirectly the cause of his incarceration. He was obliged, through self-respect, or, at least, from fear of the contempt of others, not to undervalue too much her brilliant singing. But he habitually praised other singers at her expense; especially a Mdlle. Schechner, as to whom little in the present day seems to be known, and Angelica Catalani, one of the most famous singers who ever lived. About Catalani mainly, and about Sontag incidentally, Rellstab wrote as follows in the year 1827 :—

" Mdlle. Sontag also has made a great name for herself in this piece " [the difficult variations by Rode originally composed for the violin]. " In comparing the two performances, our opinion is that, with a voice of facile flexibility like that of Mdlle. Sontag, she may well surpass her rival in certain small respects of precision, but that, on the other hand, in the delivery of the air, as well as in a general daring fluency, Mdlle. Catalani carries off the palm by a long way; not to mention the con-

scientious simplicity with which the latter singer
devotes herself to whatever may be her immediate
task, so that even songs which in themselves would
hardly please an elevated taste acquire with her a
naturalness which gives them a decided right to
exist, while, with other singers, they obtain rarely
more than mere sufferance. The relative position
of the two singers would thus be about that of a
copy in miniature compared with an original painting
in its natural dimensions."

On the 5th November, 1827, Mdlle. Sontag sang
for her benefit the principal part in *Tancredi;*
transposed for her, of course, since this part was
written by Rossini for the contralto voice.

On this occasion the King presented her with
four hundred gold pieces and two gold salvers full
of trinkets; the Princess Liegnitz gave her a gold
chain, and the Crown Princess kissed her in public.

She was about to leave Vienna for the Hague,
whence she was to make her way to Paris to fulfil
another engagement. To the Hague she carried
with her a letter of introduction from the King to
his sister, the Queen of the Netherlands. She made
a pause at Weimar in order to sing once more to
Goethe, who, as we have already seen, had written
to Zelter that he was one of those who would gladly
sit in the Königstadt Theatre " to-day, and all day "
to hear her; and who complained that " the
happiness which passes by without returning leaves

behind it an impression that may be compared to a vacuum, and is felt like a want."

From Weimar Sontag moved on to Frankfort, where she sang in public; and here it was that Ludwig Börne, who previously had been enraged at the Sontag frenzy, wrote about the fascinating singer in these enthusiastic terms :—

"My mind was full of the most indignant things, all of which I was going to publish; but since I have heard and seen the enchantress myself she has bewitched me also like the rest. Now I wish to praise her; but who will furnish me with the words? One might put a prize of a hundred ducats on the invention of an adjective that has not been used for Sontag, and none would win the prize. She has been called 'the indescribable, the heavenly, the incomparable, the divine, the universally admired, the matchless, the adorable, the adored, the delicate pearl, the dear Henriette, sweetest of maidens, darling little girl, the heroine of song, divine child, the champion of melody, the pride of Germany, the pearl of opera.' I approve of all these epithets with all my heart. To praise our singer let me speak of the frenzy which she has caused here; for such universal intoxication, if it does no credit to the toper, does at least to the wine. Henriette Sontag might, with a slight alteration, say like Cæsar, 'Veni, vidi, vici!' Victory went before her, and the fight was merely a game for the glorification of the victory. The landlord of the hotel in which Fräulein Sontag had lived for a fort-night refused, on her departure, to accept any pay-ment, and in acting so he raised and rejuvenated the old ' Römische Kaiser' into a Prytaneum in which illustrious Germans of the Fatherland are enter-tained. Visitors flocked up in great numbers from long distances : even from Cologne and Hanover the strangers came pouring in."

At Frankfort the music of Mdlle. Sontag's voice produced, together with much happiness, some misery. Several persons fainted during the per-formances, and one man went home and died. This, however, was not the result of spiritual ecstasy, but of bodily pressure.

Either at the Hague or at Paris Mdlle. Sontag made the acquaintance of Count Rossi, Sardinian Ambassador, accredited to the Hague ; whom soon afterwards she was to marry. Among her warmest admirers were many who must be considered better judges than the wilful-minded Saphir; Rossini, for instance, Cherubini, Boieldieu, Auber, and Paer.

Early in 1828 Mdlle. Sontag visited London, where she was received with such homage as was rarely in those days offered to professional vocalists. It is known that at private parties the singers engaged to contribute to the entertainment of the company used to be separated from the invited guests by a silken cord, which kept them in a fold of their own.

Every foreign musician who has published memoirs concerning the England of fifty or sixty years ago (the offensive custom may have lasted until a still later time) has called attention to the insular peculiarity by which singers and musicians of the highest artistic position were thus isolated. Rossini was never restrained by the silken cord, neither was Spohr. But Spohr in his reminiscences speaks of it, and tells how when he visited a great house he caused himself to be announced like any other visitor, and how he ignored altogether the tightly-drawn boundary line.

Sontag, too, was spared the humiliation of the rope; which, when one thinks of it, the singers who submitted to it for that very reason deserved. The French Ambassador, Prince Polignac, introduced her formally at all the best houses. In reference to the impression made by Mdlle. Sontag at a ball given by the Duke of Devonshire, Goethe, who continued to think not only of her singing but of herself as " a sweet agreeable enjoyment," received a letter from a correspondent in London, which contained this passage :—

" Fräulein Sontag danced with a special grace. The most fashionable world crowded around her anxious to hear a few words from her lips. This is a distinction without example in London."

Moscheles was at this time in England; and he tells us in his diary " that from the day of her arrival,

April 3rd, she was the cause of endless pleasant and sweet enjoyment. The charming young lady," he continues, " independently of her talent, was most seductive and fascinating in her appearance. Free from presumption or caprice, she came and went everywhere. Nay, when she is seated at our own domestic table we entirely forget that London looks forward to her *début* with intense interest. To-day, in the great rehearsal of *Barbiere*, she enraptured everyone in her part of ' Rosina.' When she showed herself on the balcony her lovely appearance was greeted with applause ; when she entered the stage with her ' Una voce poco fa ' her voice and singing enthralled everybody. Never did a shadow fall upon her London performances. The throng in the stalls of the Opera-house (where the ticket costs only a guinea) was so great that gentlemen arrived at their seats without their coat-tails, ladies without their head-dresses. I could not tell which of her representations I considered the most successful ; for her singing is always enchanting, and although I am conscious of the absence of the greater dramatic effects, still, the naturalness and sweetness of her play and appearance during the performance occupies one's attention too much to allow one to miss anything. Even when she sings her variations upon the ' Schweizerbue ' it never occurs to me, ' How does she manage to gurgle thus ? ' For her performance is perfect in its way."

" At the grand dinner which Prince Esterhazy gave in honour of Mdlle. Sontag there were present Prince and Princess Polignac, Baron Bülow, Count Redern, Lord Hertford, and Lord and Lady Ellenborough. Mdlle. Sontag sang in the most enchanting manner at night. That the Duke of Devonshire soon afterwards invited Fräulein Sontag to his ball, and even danced with her, caused great sensation at the time. The charming young lady wore that evening a very transparent dress of white crape, to which a trimming of genuine gold braiding gave a classical character; her sweet appearance was heightened still more by the handsome gold ornaments she wore in her hair and around her finely modelled neck and perfect arms and hands.

" Once we had the good fortune to see our sweet celebrated countrywoman among us in a somewhat numerous company; she was enchanting, worthy of love; her ways, her singing, everything called forth admiration. Walter Scott, who happened to be in London at the time, had paid us a visit. He was delighted to meet Sontag, and she, who was just about to appear in the *Donna del Lago*, considered herself very fortunate to make the acquaintance of the youthful old man. He was all ears and eyes when she asked him about her costume as a Highland lass. He described to her every fold of the plaid with that minuteness peculiar to him. I may mention besides that 'Jettel' had among us two fervent admirers; the other was Clementi, not less enraptured than Scott. He flourished with the freshness of youth. But now you should have seen how the two hoary old men, Scott and Clementi, were delighted with one another, shook hands, and in spite of each other's courting of and admiration for Sontag showed no mutual jealousy."

After spending some months in London, Mdlle. Sontag went once more to Paris; and here it soon became rumoured that she was engaged, if not secretly married, to Count Rossi.

The most interesting event in Mdlle. Sontag's life is her marriage. The French, little acquainted with the fortune of the prima donna in England, where from the earliest times dukes, marquises, and earls have eagerly sought her hand, were startled by the news that the singer they adored had received an offer from an Italian nobleman, who was not only a Count, but Ambassador of his Government in foreign parts. Mdlle. Sontag's favoured admirer was the representative of Sardinia at Frankfort, capital of the now extinct Germanic Confederation, where he was the doyen or senior member of the diplomatic body. In our own time a prima donna may marry any number of Ambassadors. Miss Victoria Balfe, for instance, became the wife, first of Sir John Crampton, English Ambassador at St. Petersburg, and afterwards of the Duke de Frias, Spanish Ambassador at Paris: and our readers already know that in the infant days of opera, marriage with a first-class nobleman was, in England at least, the ordinary termination of a prima donna's career. Thus, to speak of English vocalists alone, Miss Anastasia Robinson became Countess of Peterborough; Miss Lavinia Fenton, Duchess of Bolton; while at a later period Miss Stephens became Countess of Essex; Miss Foote, Countess of Harrington; Miss Bolton, Lady Thurlow; Miss Clara Novello, Countess Gigliucci.

On the continent, however, in those benighted days, men of many quarterings hesitated, and were made to hesitate, before contracting marriage with a woman recommended by nothing but her genius, her beauty, and, possibly, her virtue ; and there was much talk and infinite speculation as to the relations between Count Rossi and Mademoiselle Sontag before their marriage was actually celebrated. To make things pleasant for his favourite vocalist and prepare her gradually for the exalted position to which she was to be raised, the King of Prussia ennobled Mademoiselle Sontag by the name and title of von Lauenstein.

The brilliant prima donna was now worthy of being married, even to a Sardinian Count. But still her friends, those, at least, of the musical world, could not believe that she would desert them and forsake her art in order to become an Ambassadress. The situation inspired Scribe with the subject of a lyrical drama, which Auber set to music, and which was brought out at the Opéra Comique under the title of *L'Ambassadrice.* In this work the artistic heroine is represented as on the point of becoming the wife of a great nobleman; when, at the last moment, disgusted at the obstacles thrown in the way of the union, she tears up the permission to marry, obtained after much delay from the King, and taking an abrupt farewell of her would-be husband, returns impulsively to the lyric stage.

As a matter of fact Mdlle. Sontag forsook the Opera; and when *L'Ambassadrice* was produced she was already married to Count Rossi. The Ambassador, however, having but little private fortune, his wife continued for a time to sing, first on the stage and afterwards for a brief period at concerts only. Rellstab had, by the year 1830, become completely reconciled to the heroine of the "Zuschaner" pamphlet; and of her last operatic performance, May 22nd, 1830, he wrote in these enthusiastic terms :—

"The third representation of the opera *Semiramide* was the last in which Mdlle. Sontag (who by this time has left our town) appeared. The great tension and elevation which every solemn movement gives to our strength seemed also to produce its effect on the rich talent of our artist, and to animate her to an unwonted performance, accustomed though we are to her always remarkable representations.

Her whole conception and execution of the part suggests a beautiful stream with luxuriant banks, which, from its source to its mouth, discloses perpetually new charms to our eyes. A loud, continuous applause, or that higher approval which announces itself by anxious expectation in one's breast, that dominates all listeners, and produces the profoundest silence, testified to the power of art in penetrating every soul. One looked forward with a kind of fear to the conclusion, when this admirable singing would perhaps cease for ever, and the fair performer disappear from the scene of her mighty activity to return no more. The curtain fell. All seemed desirous to show her once more the entire breadth of the enthusiasm which her talent had kindled. The applause that shook the house was indescribable, intermingled with the vociferous calling of her name. The curtain rose again. She stood before us. She was about to withdraw when Herr Bader appeared with a wreath in his hand, and in the name of the Muse of Song addressed a few words to her, whilst, at the same time, from the other side, there entered Mdlle. Wolff, who with significant emphasis offered to her the homage of the Muses who protect histrionic art. The whole of the vast assembly was bound to share this acknowledgment, as well as the wishes and expressions of homage contained in the various poetical effusions showered down upon her."

On this occasion the King of Prussia presented Mdlle. Sontag, as once before, with four hundred gold pieces. Although it was now perfectly well known that Mdlle. Sontag had become the Countess Rossi, the Count did not publicly announce the marriage until after his wife (in 1830) had made a very lucrative concert tour. From Frankfort Count Rossi was transferred to St. Petersburg; and here, at the request of the Emperor Nicholas, who constantly invited her not only to the Court, but to the intimate society of the members of the Imperial family, Sontag appeared, before the Court only, in some of her most famous impersonations. This is said to have led to an animated correspondence between the Courts of St. Petersburg and Turin. The King of Sardinia had declared that the conduct of his Ambassador's wife in recalling too vividly her prenuptial occupation was "unbecoming." The Emperor Nicholas, on the other hand, objected to the word "unbecoming," inasmuch as nothing could be "unbecoming" which was done at his request.

Eighteen years after her marriage, in the revolutionary year of 1848, the Countess Rossi was obliged to return to the stage. Sardinia had been ruined by Carlo Alberto's heroic but unsuccessful contest with Austria; and with Sardinia fell Count Rossi, one of her most important public functionaries. Sardinia had to pay the expenses of the war, and the

Sardinian Ambassadors or Ministers abroad were recalled and replaced by *chargés d'affaires* at much lower salaries. Under these circumstances the Countess Rossi caused inquiries to be made in London, through her devoted friend Lord Westmoreland, then British Ambassador at Berlin, as to what terms Mr. Lumley, manager of Her Majesty's Theatre, would be disposed to offer her. Mr. Lumley, whose operatic experiences did not go back nearly so far as the year 1828, began by making inquiries as to what the famous singer of twenty years previously had since become. He was assured that during the long period which had elapsed since her retirement from the stage the Countess Rossi had grown a little older, but that neither her voice nor her figure had suffered in any perceptible manner from the freaks and ravages of time. Bearing this in mind, it also occurred to Mr. Lumley that even if Mdlle. Sontag had perchance lost some of the qualities of her voice, she had certainly gained in social attractiveness, and that never before had an Ambassadress been seen on the stage.

For a time there seemed to be some possibility that the Countess Rossi would not find herself forced to resume her operatic career. She herself wrote to Mr. Lumley to that effect. She had received an offer of £6,000 for one season, and in acknowledging it used these words:—" When Herr Thalberg was here everything seemed to indicate that I should soon be able to accept your offer. However, political events seemed to have somewhat consolidated the position of Piedmont since then, and you will understand that in such a moment I must not come to a resolution which only absolute necessity could justify."

Thalberg, who for a season or two was Mr. Lumley's musical conductor, had been carrying on with the Countess Rossi the negotiations first opened by Lord Westmoreland. A few days later the Countess Rossi again wrote to Mr. Lumley. " I am quite sensible," she said, " of the great difficulty and unpleasantness of your position, and I should be glad indeed if it were in my power to end this wretched uncertainty. But no doubt also you will understand with what difficulties we have to deal, and with what delicacy to act. As soon as I am once more Mdlle. Sontag your interests shall be wholly mine; to you I shall devote myself with heart and soul."

There were other delays, however, before a final resolution could be arrived at. In the end the defeat of Novara had really the effect of sending Mdlle. Sontag back to the operatic stage. She reappeared in *Linda di Chamouni*, one of Donizetti's latest works; his latest, indeed, of all, with the exception of his last comic opera, *Don Pasquale* (Paris, 1843), and his last serious opera, *Maria di Rohan* (Vienna, 1843). *Linda di Chamouni* was written for Vienna

in 1842, and although in 1848 it was already known
in England, it was still a comparative novelty.

Coming just after Jenny Lind, Mdlle. Sontag (as
she once more called herself) met with the greatest
success; and she was as much admired in private as
the Countess Rossi as on the stage under her less
aristocratic but more illustrious name.   After
" Linda " she appeared successively as " Rosina,"
in the *Barber of Seville;* " Amina," in the *Sonnambula;* " Desdemona," in *Otello;* and " Susanna," in
Figaro, chiefly, that is to say, in parts now regarded
as belonging to the " light soprano " voice; though,
when Mdlle. Sontag first appeared on the stage the
distinction was not known.   It is apparently attributable to Meyerbeer, who, in each of his four grand
operas, has two heroines, to one of whom is assigned
music of an expressive and dramatic character, to
the other music of a light and airy kind.

For Mdlle. Sontag's second season Mr. Lumley
had invited Halévy to compose an opera on the subject of Shakespeare's *Tempest,* and *La Tempesta*
was the result, with Mdlle. Sontag in the part
of " Miranda."   Halévy's opera was not a great
success, though the ballet music was much admired,
especially one number in which Arne's " Where the
bee sucks " was introduced.   The year following,
1850, Mdlle. Sontag made her first reappearance in
Paris.   Of her wonderful success at the Théâtre des

Italiens an account is given by Gustav zu Putlitz in his "Theatrical Reminiscences."

"The event caused an unusual amount of expectation, and a keen discussion of the hazardous enterprise, although Countess Rossi had proved already in London that she was still the first singer of the world in her line. This very proof given in foreign parts made the Parisians distrustful. The people there want to be makers of their own enthusiasm; nay, more, they arrogantly usurp the pretension that without the Paris stamp of recognition there exists no celebrity at all. We, the German countrymen of the singer, had often to break a lance on her account, owing to this Parisian incredulity; thus it was natural enough that we all wished to be present at the first performance. It was impossible to obtain tickets for the opening night of the Italian season, so we had been forced to look forward to the following nights; but I, who was to leave Paris the next day, saw every prospect cut off, perhaps for life, of seeing this prodigy of the stage, whose loud ovations had rung in my ears when a child, and who now, like a long-hidden treasure, was raised once more to the light to be seen, heard, and admired. That made my departure from Paris more trying still."

Then, as now, the country for an operatic singer to make money in was America; and thither in the spring of 1854 went Mdlle. Sontag. She had not, however, been many weeks in the land where she had hoped for golden rewards, when she was carried off by cholera. She died in Mexico, June 17th, 1854, to be remembered in operatic history as the only German singer, who, up to that time, had gained a great European reputation.

She had often expressed a wish to be buried one day in the Convent where her sister Nina was a nun, and this wish was now fulfilled. The remains of Henriette Sontag were conveyed by steamer up the Elbe, and buried near Dresden in the Convent of St. Marienthal. On the lid of her coffin was this inscription :—

" To the best of mothers. To the tenderest of daughters. To the most faithful wife. To the noblest friend. To the greatest singer."

CHAPTER XI.

MALIBRAN.

DAUGHTER of Garcia, the original "Almaviva" of Rossini's *Barbiere*, Marietta Malibran is also connected with operatic history as sister of Madame Viardot Garcia, the unrivalled "Fidès" of Meyerbeer's *Prophète*, and the only "Orfeo" of these latter days. How the Garcia children used to be bullied by their tyrant father has often been told. He would beat them until they screamed; and so little after a time did their cries affect the people in the neighbourhood, that when shrieks of unusual volume and acuteness proceeded from the house (they were living in Paris at the time) passers-by would say: "It is nothing; it is only Monsieur Garcia teaching his daughters to sing."

The most cruel act, however, of Garcia towards his daughter Marietta was not committed until she had attained her seventeenth year, when in 1825 he gave her to an old and profligate merchant named

Malibran. French by nationality and American by settlement, Malibran had scarcely married the idolized prima donna when he became bankrupt. He had in his boundless mendacity promised Garcia a present of one hundred thousand francs; and perhaps the only satisfactory point connected with the shameful marriage was the non-fulfilment of this engagement.

The French courts, by some process not wholly intelligible (for divorce was at that time impossible in France), are said to have annulled the marriage. In any case, Madame Malibran became some time afterwards the wife apparent of De Bériot, the famous Belgian violinist. According to Moscheles, Malibran's first marriage was dissolved by special dispensation from the Pope.

Moscheles, as is well pointed out in his interesting "Life," had abundant opportunities of judging youthful talent; for fathers and mothers brought him their youthful prodigies, most of whom have vanished and are now forgotten. But more than with all other wonders in the way of musical children he was charmed with the youthful, almost childish, actress, Marietta Garcia, afterwards Malibran, whom he saw for the first time on an amateur stage in the house of a M. Hallmandel. "The charming girl," he writes, " almost a child, acted enchantingly in the *Chauvin de Rheims, Le Coin de Rue,* and *L'Ours et le Pacha.*" At the same time he was delighted with the dramatic singing of her father, who was one of the greatest tenors of his day.

No one has given a fuller or more interesting account of Malibran than Moscheles, whose writings and sayings concerning this charming artist must always be referred to by those who wish to gain a true knowledge of her character, whether as an artist or as a woman. I may here, however, observe, on the authority of a contributor to a well-written musical journal, published from fifty-five to sixty years ago, under the title of *The Harmonicon,* that Malibran was less successful in oratorio than in opera. " Concerning Madame Malibran," says the critic in question, in a notice of the Liverpool Musical Festival of 1830, " of whom, in all probability, we shall have neither occasion nor opportunity to speak again for some time to come, a few words at parting. We repeat, then, that in Handel's music she has made no favourable impression upon us ; and at all our festivals we think we may safely affirm she has succeeded best in her Provençal airs. But, in justice, let us add that, to form a proper estimate of Madame Malibran's talent, she must be seen and heard on the opera stage ; and notwithstanding her whim, caprice, and eccentricity, with which, it is said, she abounds even to overflowing, we consider her to be a most extraordinary and highly talented creature."

Once at Drury Lane Theatre Moscheles joined

Malibran and other stars in a concert, which began after the opera, and lasted till midnight. Balfe had just produced, with great success, his first English opera, *The Siege of Rochelle* : " the music light, after the manner of the composer himself, but cheerful and pleasing like him." After this Balfe wrote for Malibran *The Maid of Artois*. The versatile artist, equally at home in the English, Italian, French, and Spanish languages, was engaged as prima donna at Drury Lane Theatre. " Did Balfe," asks Moscheles, "intend her to do battle with those incredibly difficult passages at the beginning, or were they improvised by her on the spur of the moment? I can't say. Somehow or other the enchantress conjured them forth. I don't like her so well in ' Fidelio,' and prefer our own unrivalled Schröder-Devrient in the part. Malibran's forte lies in passionate acting, which contrasts too violently with the enduring womanly love of ' Fidelio,' and why she brings two pistols into the prison neither I nor anyone else can understand."

Malibran's protracted stay in London led to a close intimacy with the Moscheles, at whose house she was a constant visitor. " Her sparkling genius, sunny cheerfulness, and never-failing spirit " is said to have " contrasted forcibly with de Bériot's apathy, not to say coldness, more especially as the two artists were constantly seen and judged together. Other singers may captivate by their art, and gifted and amiable women by their manners and conversation; but

Malibran had magic power to lead us captives, body and soul. In Moscheles' house she had everyone at her feet; the children looked on her as their own property; she alone knew the right way to play with the dolls' house, and none other but Malibran had a certain black silk bag of irresistible attraction to the little ones. The contents of this bag were not, however, the common-place things—toys and sugar-plums—but a paint-box, paper, and brushes. She would come into the room, and the minute afterwards she would be down on the carpet with the children, letting them pull out everything, and then the picture-making began, and she would throw her whole energies into the work, and share the children's intense delight."

"I began my duty," writes Moscheles again, " by setting Goethe's ' Meeresstille und Glückliche Fahrt ' as a song for Malibran. We had great fun the other day when she and De Bériot joined our early dinner. The conversation turned upon Gnecco's comic duet, which Malibran sang so frequently and charmingly with Lablache. Man and wife ridicule and abuse one another, caricaturing alternately each other's defects. When she came to the passage ' La tua bocca è fatta apposta pel servizio della posta,' ' Just like my mouth,' said Malibran, ' as broad as you please, and I'll just put this orange in to prove it.' One must have known De Bériot to appreciate his amazement and agony at seeing his wife open her mouth wide, and discover two beautiful rows of teeth, behind which the orange disappeared. Then she roared with laughter at her successful performance.

" She came at three o'clock; with her were Thalberg, Benedict, and Klingemann. We dined early and immediately afterwards Malibran sat down to the piano and 'sang for the children,' as she used to say, the 'Rataplan' and some of her father's Spanish songs; for want of a guitar accompaniment she used, whilst playing, every now and then to mark the rhythm on the board at the back of the keys. After singing with exquisite grace and charm a number of French and Italian romances of her own composition, she was relieved at the piano by Thalberg, who performed all manner of tricks on the instrument, snapping his fingers as an obligato to Viennese songs and waltzes. I played afterwards with reversed hands, and with my fists, and none laughed louder than Malibran. At five o'clock we drove to the Zoological Gardens, and pushed our way for an hour with the fashionables. When we had had enough of man and beast we took one more turn in the Park, and directly we got home Malibran sat down to the piano and sang for an hour. At last, however, she called out to Thalberg: ' Venez jouer quelque chose, j'ai besoin de me reposer.' Her repose consisting in finishing a most charming landscape in water colours (an art in which she was self-taught). Thalberg played by heart and in a most masterly way several of his ' Studies ' and fragments of a newly-written rondo, then my ' Studies,' ' Allegri di Bravura' and 'G Minor Concerto.' We had supper afterwards ; then again it was Malibran who kept us all going. She gave us the richest imitations of Sir George Smart, the singers Knyvett, Braham, Phillips, and Vaughan, who had sung with her at a concert given by the Duchess of C—, taking off the fat Duchess herself, as she condescendingly patronized 'her' artists ; winding up with the cracked voice and nasal tones of Lady ——, she inflicted ' Home, sweet home ' on the company. Suddenly her comic vein came to a full stop ; then she gave in the thorough German style the scena from *Freyschütz*, with German words, and a whole series of German songs by Mendelssohn, Schubert, Weber, and my humble self ; lastly she took a turn with *Don Juan*, being familiar not only with the music of 'Zerlina,' her own part, but knowing by heart every note in the opera, which she could play and sing from beginning to end. She went on playing and singing alternately until eleven o'clock, fresh to the last in voice and spirits. When she left us we were all rapturous about her music, languages, painting ; but what we liked best was her artlessness and amiability."

Moscheles composed for her a song to Klingemann's words, " Steigt der Mond auf" (" The moon rises"). She made him play to her constantly, knew several of his "Studies" by heart, and said that her father had made her practise them.

Moscheles, speaking in one of his letters of a concert at his own house, adds: "Malibran and De Bériot appeared at eleven o'clock, after our eighty guests had satisfied their musical appetite with English vocal music, solos by Lipinsky and Servais, and my own 'Concert Fantastique.' She looked very weary; and when she sang one scarcely recognized Malibran, she was so voiceless. We only heard subsequently that she had been thrown from her horse when riding in the Park. Although suffering no injury she had not yet recovered from the violent shock. She was soon herself, however, and sang two *Freyschütz* scenas in German, a comic English duet with John Parry, three Spanish, Italian, and French songs, winding up with the duet, 'Cadence du Diable' for herself and De Bériot, in which she prefaces his daring and marvellous violin passages with the words: 'Voyez comme le diable prélude.' The proper name of the piece is 'Le Songe de Tartini;' and the supposition being that the master has, in a dream, seen the devil, and heard him play the piece right through, every latitude is allowed for whims and eccentricities. When my wife showed some anxiety lest she should over-exert herself, she replied, 'Ma chère, je chanterais pour vous jusqu' à extinction de voice.' It was interesting to watch her rap-

tures in listening to a duet composed and played by
Benedict and De Bériot; certain passages in the
work seemed to me possibly to have emanated from
her pen. I was called on at the end of the evening
to improvise; and, that the comic element might be
properly represented, young John Parry amused us
with his masterly parody of the scena in the 'Wolf's
Glen' in the *Freyschütz*. With a sheet of music
rolled up, with one hand in his mouth, the other
resting on the desk, he produced the deepest horn
or trombone notes; his hands worked the keys,
and his feet a tea-tray. There was the 'Wilde
Jagd' complete. Thalberg had a bad finger, and
could not play; but he and De Bériot stayed with
us until three in the morning, gossiping and com-
menting upon the events of the evening."

On the 11th May Moscheles was assisted by De
Bériot at his concert in the Italian Opera-house. "I
had an 'embarras de richesses;' besides the great star
Malibran, there were Lablache, Grisi, and Clara
Novello. I played a concerto of Bach's that had
never been heard in England, and my own 'C Minor
Concerto.' It was a tremendous success for all concerned. After a performance of the *Maid of Artois*,
in which Malibran sang marvellously, we went
to see her in her dressing-room. There she sat surrounded by wreaths and an enormous bouquet in her
hand. She talked and laughed with us, adding:
'Si vous vouliez me débarrasser de cette machine,

c'est cet abominable Duc de Brunswick qui vient de me l'apporter ; ' and so saying she threw a colossal bouquet at me, which I caught. What must ' the abominable Duke' have thought, when, a few moments later, he saw me mount my carriage and carry off his bouquet ? For so it happened at the entrance-door of Drury Lane Theatre."

The exertions of the famous artist were incessant, for, independently of her three operatic performances per week, she was constantly engaged for morning and evening concerts, and accepted all sorts of invitations to fashionable breakfasts, *fêtes champêtres*, and private parties. To attend three parties on the same evening was a matter of constant occurrence with her. "On the 16th of July," writes Moscheles, "before the De Bériots started on their journey, we spent an hour with Malibran by appointment; and found her at the piano, with Costa standing by her. She sang us a comic song that she had just composed. A sick man weary of life invokes death ; but when death, personified by a doctor, knocks at the door, he dismisses him with scorn. She had set this subject so cleverly, and sang the music so humorously, that we could scarcely refrain from laughing ; and yet we could not endure to lose a single note. After this she wrote in my album a charming French romance ; this she sang to us, and she then presented my wife with one of her original water-colour landscapes."

It seems strange in the present day when English opera can scarcely be said to exist that fifty years ago two English composers, W. M. Balfe and G. A. Macfarren, should have enjoyed the inestimable advantage of having such a singer as Malibran for the principal parts in their works. It is a fact, however, that Malibran appeared at Drury Lane, under the management of Mr. Bunn, both in Balfe's *Maid of Artois* and in the *Devil's Bridge* of Macfarren.

"At Drury Lane," writes Moscheles, "the sparkling, and in the vocal and histrionic way, unique Malibran, made a *furore* in the *Devil's Bridge* and *Sonnambula*, set to English words. She was thoroughly realistic, and in her dress and movements despised everything conventional. Thus, in the sleep-walking scene, unlike other great representatives of the part, whose muslin *négligé* would have suited any lady, she adopted the *bonâ-fide* nightcap of the peasant girl, and the loose garment of a sleeper; her *tricot* stockings were so transparent as to veil her feet but imperfectly. Her acting in this opera was exquisitely touching, her outburst of sorrow so natural that she enlisted the sympathy of her audience from beginning to end of the piece."

Macfarren, Sterndale Bennett, and James Davison —who was afterwards to turn from composition to criticism—were three of the most enthusiastic musicians of their time. They worked together, lived together, nurtured the same aspirations, entertained the same passionate admiration for the music of Mendelssohn, and equally detested in after years the music of Wagner. Sterndale Bennett once called Wagner a "Brummagem Berlioz;" Macfarren has been heard to say that his instrumentation recalled the horrors of German street bands; and if Davison at last recognized his power, he did so not from any natural sympathy, but rather by force of will, and in order to bring himself more or less into accord with the changing taste of the day. Mendelssohn's worshippers could not, indeed, be expected to be prejudiced in favour of a composer who apparently hated Mendelssohn personally, who always spoke disparagingly of his music, and who (in "Opera and Drama") writes of him that, "having nothing to say, he said it like a gentleman and disappeared." But the period of Macfarren and his friends was, above all, the period of Mendelssohn; and even if Wagner had never breathed a syllable against the reigning divinity, those who had nourished themselves on the music of the one would have been sure to find that of the other somewhat indigestible.

Moscheles, in his autobiography, expresses views with regard to Wagner's music which were those held generally by the musicians of his time and of his school. "As often," he writes, "as I hear this opera (*Don Juan*) and think of the music of the future, I feel as if I had suddenly emerged from a

dark wood, where toads and hobgoblins make a
hideous concert, and was coming forth into the
sunny light of day and Apollo playing me heavenly
melodies."

Macfarren's style in his operas and oratorios is not
particularly Mendelssohnian. It is a mixed style,
in which, however, there is a good deal of his own.
The present generation knows little or nothing of
Macfarren as an operatic composer, and considering
that he wrote his first opera half a century ago,
and that more than a quarter of a century has
passed since his last was produced, this is natural.
His works, it is true, might have been revived. But
they never made sufficient mark to warrant any
such hazardous process; and for a long time past,
moreover, we have had no permanent operatic establishment in London. Otherwise, Sir George Macfarren's *Robin Hood*, which bears the comparatively
recent date of 1860, and possibly his *Charles II.*,
which belongs to a still earlier time, could have
been performed any time during the last few years
with more success than has attended the representation of a good many original works by composers
of the present day; though this, after all, is saying
very little. It must be added that even when they
were first brought out these operas never attained
anything like the popularity achieved from a whole
series of works from the facile pen of Balfe; nor
did they meet with such applause as was freely

bestowed on Wallace's *Maritana,* or on the same composer's *Lurline* and *Amber Witch.* Indeed, as regards his place in public favour (no absolute criterion, it must be admitted), Macfarren would have to be ranked below Benedict, whose *Lily of Killarney* obtained a far greater number of representations than was reached by any of Macfarren's operas. The *Lily of Killarney,* moreover, stood the test of a revival at the hands of Mr. Carl Rosa, and stood it well. It must, however, be remembered on behalf of Macfarren that in most of his operas he had but a poor libretto to work upon; whereas Balfe, in the *Bohemian Girl,* thanks to Cervante's *Gipsy of Madrid,* from which the plot is taken; Wallace in *Maritana,* with a story borrowed from *Don Cæsar de Bazan,* and Benedict in the *Lily of Killarney,* of which the theme is identical with that of the *Colleen Bawn,* had (poetry apart) good dramatic books to deal with.

Macfarren was never fortunate in his libretto but once, when Oxenford furnished him with the well-constructed, well-written music-drama of *Robin Hood.* The subject, too, of *Robin Hood* was a national one, and could be treated with that observance of character and colour which, at least in his later days, Macfarren regarded as essential to operatic success; though, except in *Robin Hood,* he cannot anywhere be said to have followed these precepts of his own making, or, at least, of his own adoption. In *Robin Hood*, moreover, Macfarren enjoyed the further advantage of having the principal part sung by the first English tenor of our time. Had he been provided with a succession of good opera books, Macfarren might, if there had been an operatic theatre to write for, have produced a whole series of lyric dramas ; and it was in this department of his art, as his intimate friends well know, that he particularly desired to excel. But to make in England a practical study of the art of composing operas is as difficult to become a navigator in Switzerland or a skater in India.

The period of Sir George Macfarren will seem to many composers of the present day rather a dark one. Yet both he and Sterndale Bennett wrote symphonies and overtures which Mendelssohn thought worthy of being produced at his Leipsic concerts ; and we know from the writings of Schumann, whose authority cannot be disregarded, that they were accepted by the musical public of Germany as possessing high merit. Apart, however, from Bennett and Macfarren, the composers of that period show points of inferiority compared with those who are prominent in the present day. The operas which that bad poet, but able manager, Mr. Alfred Bunn, used to produce in very considerable numbers were slight, slender works, viewed by the side of the formidable ones which are now produced for the most part in a stillborn condition. The

musical dramas of Sir George Macfarren's period—
furnished as they were with overtures instead of
"preludes," with at least one or two set songs for
each of the principal characters, and with formal
concerted pieces, each complete in itself — used
somehow, in spite of their old-fashioned peculiarities, to exist; and this, in connection with works
addressed to the general public and intended to
please it, is in itself a merit. The founder of
a new system of philosophy or of a new school
of poetry may disregard the question of immediate
success; but the dramatic composer, equally with
the dramatist whose characters use the speaking
voice, is bound under the penalty of absolute failure
to interest the hearers of his own time.

Mr. Carl Rosa, in an article on the general
subject of English operas, has pointed out that
most operatic composers, even in the case of
those who were afterwards to obtain brilliant
success, have begun with failures; and the same
may be said of dramatists generally. Two of the
most successful dramatists of modern times—Scribe
in Sir George Macfarren's day and Sardou in our
own—wrote several unsuccessful plays before finding (so to say) their stage legs; and when a
composer skilled in all the resources of his art
has failed in a line to which he has not been
accustomed, it would be unjust, and, indeed, absurd
to say that in this very line he will not, after

further experiments, greatly distinguish himself. One thing, meanwhile, is certain : that from thirty to fifty or fifty-five years ago (which carries us back to about the beginning of Balfe's career) our operatic composers, whether greater men or not than those of the present day, had far greater opportunities.

Many works produced by Mr. Bunn and Mr. Maddox—for there was a time when we had two English Operas playing night after night for months together—would not find favour in the eyes of a modern manager ; nor even if any manager should venture to produce them would there be much chance of their satisfying the public ; for our public has improved in musical taste. Mr. Carl Rosa, when he was still new, at least in England, to the work of management, revived Balfe's *Siege of Rochelle*, which had enjoyed great popularity in its day ; but it soon appeared that the work belonged altogether to a bygone age. It was not until he saw that there was no Opera-house to write for that, like so many other English composers, Macfarren gave himself up to the composition of oratorios ; and the history of Macfarren's oratorios has been the ordinary one of a single performance at some provincial festival, one performance, or, by rare good fortune, two, in London, and then oblivion. Yet undoubtedly he has left his mark in the history of music in England ; and though his works (with the exception, perhaps, of his little book on " Harmony ") may be forgotten, he himself will be remembered. He possessed a full knowledge of the science of his art and of the works which that art has produced, and he exercised powerful influence, not only on all who studied under him, but on all who approached him.

It has been said that Moscheles heard Malibran in the *Devil's Bridge ;* but he confines himself to mentioning the bare fact, without giving any account of the work. Neither of Macfarren's opera nor of Malibran's singing in it does he speak in any detail.

Of Malibran's goodness of heart an interesting example has been recorded by Sir Julius Benedict.

" Malibran made me give my first annual concert," said Benedict one day to his friend Willert Beale. " I hesitated to incur the risk it involved, but Malibran and her husband, De Bériot, said they would pay any loss there might be; and they announced the concert in my name. The tickets were numbered and sold by Malibran herself, and I was not allowed to discontinue my lessons to attend to any of the arrangements, all of which were carried out by my two kind friends. The concert proved a great success, and De Bériot gave me forty pounds as the result. After the season I went to Paris, where I remained a few weeks, and came to terms with Troupenas, the publisher, for the publication of my compositions. When taking leave of Troupenas, before returning to London, he handed me one hundred pounds sterling, left with him for me by Malibran and De Bériot. It was the balance of the concert money. They thought that as a young man I might have squandered it had I received the whole of the amount in a lump sum, and now wished me to have it in case I had any purchases to make before leaving Paris."

"Malibran was a very gifted singer," remarked Willert Beale.

"Perhaps the most gifted I ever knew," replied Sir Julius. "Her voice was of the most extraordinary compass and of splendid quality throughout. She sang with wonderful dramatic fire and brilliancy. Nothing has ever exceeded the effect she produced in Balfe's *Maid of Artois*, the finale to which and the *fioriture* with which it was embellished gave full scope to the phenomenal extent of her power of vocalization."

"And De Bériot, her husband, was a first-rate violinist, was he not?"

"They were two incomparable artists. I cannot speak of them with sufficient gratitude, for to them, and to Malibran especially, I owe my position in this country."

"And to your own merit!"

"Whatever that may be, it would have been worth nothing without the encouragement I received at their hands fifty years ago."

Malibran's favourite characters were "Amina,"
"Norma," and "Romeo;" all, it will be observed,
personages in operas by Bellini. "The actions of
this fiery existence," says M. Castil Blaze, "would
appear fabulous if we had not seen Marietta among
us; fulfilling her engagements at the theatre, resist-
ing all the fatigue of the rehearsals, of the representations, after galloping morning and evening in the
Bois de Boulogne, so as to tire out two horses. She
used to breakfast during the rehearsals on the stage.
I said to her one morning at the theatre : ' Marietta
carissima, non morrai.' ' Che farò dunque ? Ne-
mica sorte! Creperai.' Her travels, her excursions,
her studies, her performances, might have filled the
lives of two artists, and two very complete lives,
moreover. She starts for Sinigaglia, during the heat
of July, in man's clothes, takes her seat on the box
of the carriage, drives the horses; scorched by the
sun of Italy, covered with dust, she arrives, jumps
into the sea, swims like a dolphin, and then goes to
her hotel to dress. At Brussels she is applauded as
a French "Rosina," delivering the prose of Beaumarchais as Mademoiselle Mars would have delivered
it. She leaves Brussels for London, comes back to
Paris, travels about in Brie, and returns to London,
not like a courier, but like a dove on the wing. We
all know what the life of a singer is in the capital of
England—the life of a dramatic singer of the highest
talent. After a rehearsal at the opera she may have

three or four *matinées* to attend, and when the curtain falls, and she can escape from the theatre, there are *soirées* which last till daybreak. Malibran kept all these engagements, and, moreover, gave Sunday to her friends. This day of absolute rest to all England was to Marietta only another day of excitement."

No great singer met with a more tragic end than poor Malibran—already briefly related in the citation given above from Moscheles. She had been engaged to sing at the Manchester Festival of September, 1836, and when she arrived to fulfil her engagement was already a little indisposed. Some weeks before she had been thrown from her horse, and had received an injury in the head. Unwilling, indeed afraid,* to mention the accident to her husband, who had forbidden her to get on horseback, she went over to Brussels, returned to England, and here sang and mixed in society according to her restless, indefatigable habit. When the time for her appearance at the Manchester Festival arrived she sang admirably. The enthusiasm of the audience was at its height; and, excited by the applause, Malibran, in a duet with Madame Caradori Allan—a piece from the now forgotten *Andronico* of Mercadante—eclipsed all her previous

---

* So I have been assured by the late Sir Julius Benedict, who knew Malibran intimately and remembered well all the incidents of her last days.

efforts, and at the same time exerted herself to such an extent, that at the conclusion of the performance she went into convulsions and fell shrieking to the ground.

Doctors were sent for, the inevitable lancet of the period was produced, and the poor woman was bled. Then she was carried to her hotel; and the next day she felt sufficiently recovered to return to the scene of the festival performances, and again to sing. The phlebotomists of the night before did not apparently think it necessary to forbid this most imprudent act; or it may be that the impulsive Malibran was beyond control. She, in any case, sang; and a relapse naturally enough followed. After a couple of days a certain Doctor Belluomini arrived from London; and on seeing him the enfeebled but still highly animated singer called out: " I am a slain woman; they have bled me!"

Dr. Belluomini was a homœopathist, and though he might not have cured her he certainly would not have " slain " his patient by bleeding her. The two local practitioners retired; but the case was already hopeless, and the finest singer of her time died, as the medical report said, of nervous fever; but, as Molière would probably have put it, " of two doctors and a lancet."

Before the unhappy Malibran was dead her husband had already given directions about her burial; a piece of foresight which was obligingly explained by Dr. Belluomini, who declared that when all hope was over he had told De Bériot, half an hour before the fatal end, that his wife had ceased to breathe. He had done so, he said, by reason of De Bériot's dangerous excitement, and because for many days and nights he had taken neither rest nor food.

What was still more strange, the doctor and the disconsolate husband hired a post-chaise and started for London immediately after the poor woman's death, leaving friends at Manchester—and especially the members of the festival committee—to manage the funeral. According to a correspondent of the *Morning Post*, understood to have been the late Mr. C. L. Gruneisen, the body was shown to the curious on payment of money ; though this was denied by the proprietor of the hotel, who declared that all applications to see the corpse, to make a cast of the features, to sketch the dead singer in her coffin, and so on, were met with a positive refusal. If the showing of the body for money was ever done, this indignity (which may have suggested to M. Feydau one of the most cynical scenes in his *Mari de la Danseuse*) must have been due to the servants and to shameless persons offering them bribes.

The London newspapers, indignant at De Bériot's conduct in abandoning the body of his unhappy wife to the care of strangers, demanded an explanation ; and a very lame one was furnished by Dr. Belluomini, who wrote to say that De Bériot had left

Manchester by his direction and under his care ; that his grief had been too great for him to remain ; and that though his conduct might to Englishmen seem strange, he had only followed the custom observed in his own country and in the greater part of the Continent!

In England De Bériot's heartless and indecent flight was explained by a determination to save Malibran's property before any claims to it could be put forward by her relations.

CHAPTER XII.

"These are your little Grisettes," said the Emperor Nicholas to Madame Grisi, meeting her one day at St. Petersburg, with her two little girls, Rita and Clelia. The third daughter, now Mrs. Godfrey Pearse, who tells the story, was not yet born.

"No, Sire," answered Madame Grisi, with an appropriateness almost too happy for reality; "they are my little Marionettes."

The children, who were at once "Marionettes" and "Grisettes," had for parents the greatest tenor and the greatest dramatic soprano of their time; and the two eminent vocalists seem to have been pre-destined to come together long before the fated conjunction actually took place. They sang apart for several years. But when they had once met they were not afterwards to be separated except by death. What, however, is particularly noticeable in their early lives, is that a similar adverse wind drove them at the same time from Italy to France at a period when neither knew of the other's existence and when both were unknown to fame.

Madame Grisi I knew only in her character of dramatic vocalist, but I met Mario twice in private; once at the first marriage of Madame Adelina Patti, when, with darkened hair and moustache, he might have been described as an elderly young man; and once, after he had retired from the stage, at Drury Lane Theatre, on the occasion of some Italian benefit performance, when with white hair and beard, but with eyes as black and as bright as ever, he seemed to me a singularly youthful elderly man. Although a good many years had passed since I had first seen him, I found him, notwithstanding the lapse of time, better looking in his natural than in his previous artificial condition; and I was particularly struck by the contrast between his snow-white hair and his coal black eyes. He had lost nothing of his vivacity, and his general demeanour was as light-hearted as ever.

But if I knew very little of Mario in his private character, and nothing whatever of Grisi, my old and valued friend, Willert Beale, knew them both quite intimately; and from what he has himself told me, and from what in various odd corners he has written on the subject, I am enabled to communicate much interesting information about them which has the advantage of being on all points absolutely authentic. "I knew them from my childhood," wrote Willert Beale, just after Mario's death. "Giulia Grisi taught me Italian at her knee even before I could speak my mother tongue. I had been their youngest, and became, as years rolled by, one of their oldest friends. We were constantly associated socially and in business matters. They were indeed an incomparable pair; more liberally endowed by nature with every attribute of personal beauty, vocal power, and dramatic genius than any other of their kind. Their union was an inestimable gain to art, and their attachment to one another as romantic and devoted as that of any hero and heroine they ever impersonated. It hallowed and was hallowed by their common pursuit in life; it sanctified their home, it gave incessantly renewed fire and zest to their representations upon the lyric stage."

Mario and Grisi were nearly, if not exactly, of the same age; and they were both born in the year 1810. Of the strange fatality which drove them both from Italy at the same time I have already spoken. Don Giovanni Batista di Candia (to call "Mario" by his true name) was a son of General Stefano di Candia, Governor of Nice, and a lineal descendant of Pope Alexander VI., through a brother of Lucrezia Borgia, by whom the name of "Di Candia" was first borne. Thus his exclamation in the opera: "Sono un Borgia!" had more meaning than might have been supposed. The future "Mario" was serving as an officer in the light infantry of the Sardinian Royal Guard when he suddenly became suspected of Carbonarism. Whether affiliated to the famous secret society or not, he was sentenced by his military superiors to imprisonment in a fortress. On being liberated he challenged a fellow-officer, whom he apparently suspected of having informed against him; and afterwards, to escape the consequences of the duel, fled from Italy.

Mario left Genoa for Marseilles in a fishing smack, and he was seventeen days at sea; during which time he suffered greatly, first, from storms of the most formidable character, secondly, when the stock of provisions had been exhausted, from hunger. From Marseilles he had intended to make his way to Spain; but he met with some friends who urged him to go to Paris. There accordingly he went; and he was warmly received on his arrival by Prince Belgioso, the Marquis Aguado, and others whom he already knew, or to whom he carried letters of introduction.

Grisi, meanwhile, after "creating" with signal success at Milan the part of "Adalgisa" to Pasta's "Norma," had rebelled against her director, and thereupon determined to leave Italy and seek her fortune in France. She could not, however, throw up her engagement with impunity; and, to escape the consequences of her daring act, she had to hasten in all secrecy to the frontier. Her journey across the Alps, through Switzerland, into France, at the beginning of a very severe winter, lasted twelve days, and was attended with considerable danger. But on reaching Paris she was received by her elder sister, Giuditta, who was fulfilling an engagement as prima donna at the Théâtre des Italiens, then under the direction of Rossini. Such a singer as Giulia Grisi could not fail to be appreciated by such a musician as Rossini; and the services of the newly-arrived vocalist were at once secured. On the 13th of October, 1832, she appeared for the first time before the Parisians in the part of " Semiramide;" and, in spite of the day being the thirteenth of the month (for both she and Mario were very superstitious on such points), sang with the most distinguished success. It may here be noticed that Grisi never again sang in Italy; also that Mario never sang in Italy at all.

Mario's first idea, on finding himself a gentleman at large, was to continue his military life; and being presented in London to the Duke of Wellington he asked permission to enter the British army. The Duke promised to see what he could do for him. But nothing seems to have been done; and, returning to Paris, Mario was introduced by the Marquis Aguado to Meyerbeer, who gave him lessons in sing-ing—the only ones he ever received—and soon after-wards assigned to him the part of " Raimbaud " in *Robert le Diable,* then on the point of being produced.

Unwilling to appear on the stage under his true name, Don Giovanni di Candia searched his memory and exercised his imagination in quest of a suitable appellation. At last he recollected an historical incident which connected his family with Monte Mario at Rome, and forthwith decided that as Mario he would go before the public. His pronunciation of French was at this time so defective that the Parisian audience, caring but little for his charming voice and fine style, were very near hissing him. Thus, as he himself observed long afterwards, he repaid Meyerbeer's kindness by endangering seriously the success of his opera. Mario remained for two years and a half at the Paris Opera-house, during which time he made no particular impression, though it is difficult to understand how he could have failed to sing otherwise than perfectly Raimbaud's tuneful legend, " Jadis regnait en Normandie."

Whether or not Mario could sing with expression in the French language is sufficiently shown by an incident that once happened when he was singing in a drawing-room at Paris. The song was Alary's " Viens au bois ! " The first verse of this delightful romance produced, as usual, a great effect, and Mario proceeded to sing the second verse, the words of which are :

> Ah! viens au bois folle maitresse !
> Au bois sombre et mystérieux!
> Là tu pourras de ma tendresse,
> Recueilir les si doux aveux !
> Ah, viens au bois !

Suddenly a young lady, magnetized, mesmerized
—"hypnotized," as we should say in the present
day—rose from her seat and walked slowly towards the singer, exclaiming : "*Je viens!*"

Besides *Robert le Diable*, Mario appeared at the
Académie in *Le Comte Ory*, *Le Drapier*, and other
light works. He then passed from the French to
the Italian Opera, his first part at the so-called
Théâtre des Italiens being that of " Nemorino" in
L'Elisir d'amore. Grisi, meantime, was becoming
more and more popular in Paris, where, in a
social sense, she had, from her first arrival, found
herself quite at home. Her father, a retired officer
of engineers, who had served under Napoleon,
lived habitually in Paris. He had resided there, off
and on, since the first days of the Revolution, and
it is recorded in the highly interesting diary kept by
one of Mario's daughters, Mrs. Godfrey Pearse, that
he was present in the crowd which surrounded the
scaffold when Louis XVI., and again when Marie
Antoinette was executed. " I remember him well,"
writes Mrs. Godfrey Pearse, " for he only died in
February, 1870, three months after my dear mother,
at the ripe old age of ninety-five. His head was still
covered with thick white hair, cropped closely in the
French fashion ; he was a very handsome old man."
I further learn from the same diary as communicated
to Mr. Willert Beale, that the vigorous old man
married for the second time, at the age of eighty,

quite a young wife ; who died in giving birth to three
daughters, two of whom lived and are now married
and settled in Italy.

During Madame Grisi's second season at the
Théâtre des Italiens, Bellini's last opera, *I Puritani*,
was brought out with Grisi, Rubini, Tamburini, and
Lablache in the four principal parts.   Rubini in this
famous quartet was afterwards to be replaced by
Mario ; and the quartet, thus reconstructed, was later
on to be diminished, first by the retirement of Tamburini, then by the death of Lablache.

Time passed, and the quartet in *Don Pasquale*,
composed by Donizetti for the famous four, could
no longer be sung in its original perfection.   But
Grisi and Mario could still sing the concerted duet
as no two others could sing it.   They were still the
rose and the nightingale of Heine's Parisian letters :
—" The rose the nightingale among flowers, the
nightingale the rose among birds."   Grisi had at
this time been twelve years before the Paris public,
and ten years before the public of London.   Mr. N.
P. Willis heard Grisi in London on the occasion of
her first appearance at Her Majesty's Theatre in
1834, and, as he sets forth in his " Pencillings by
the Way," did not much like her.   On the other
hand, Heine heard her in the " Norina " of *Don Pasquale* at Paris in 1844, and liked her very much
indeed.   The unbounded admiration of the German
poet would probably have consoled Madame Grisi,

if she had ever troubled herself about the matter, for the limited admiration expressed by the American prose writer.

From the year 1834, when she made her first appearance in London, until the year 1861, when she retired finally from the operatic stage, Madame Grisi missed only one season in London—that of 1842. And it was a very rare thing throughout her career for illness or any other cause to prevent her from appearing. She seldom disappointed the public by her absence, and never, when she was present, by her singing. There is significance in styling such a vocalist "robust;" for there are robust sopranos as there are "robust tenors." Indeed, no one who has not really a robust constitution could stand the wear and tear which are the inevitable accompaniments—which, indeed, form the very substance—of a singer's existence.

It has been said that Mario passed from the French Opera, or Académie Royale de Musique, as it was then called, to the Italian Opera, or Théâtre des Italiens. For a time, however, this passage was by no means definite. Duprez and Rubini being both ill, he alternately replaced one in French, the other in Italian. Then, with a month of this "doubling," in a two-fold sense, he remained permanently with the Italian company, until, in the year 1839, he came to London, engaged for Her Majesty's by Mr. Lumley, and, for the first time, made the

acquaintance of Grisi. " It was on June 6th, 1839,"
writes Mrs. Godfrey Pearse, in her diary, " that they
sang together for the first time in London at Her
Majesty's Theatre. It was my father's first appearance on the English stage as ' Gennaro,' to my
mother's ' Lucrezia Borgia ; ' and from the year
1844 he became the kind and faithful companion in
life of my darling mother, whose dear name we hold
in loving memory."

Mario began his career with a splendid voice and
exquisite musical taste; but (again to quote his
daughter) " he was as yet an indifferent actor, for he
always said that he owed his acting, which afterwards became famous, to my mother's teaching.
Her dramatic genius created in him the lyric power
and passion which at first were quite wanting, but
which afterwards made him not merely supreme, but
almost alone as an operatic performer. Many a
time when elated by the enthusiastic applause of the
audience for some piece of acting which he himself
thought very good, my mother would cool down his
ardour by saying—' It was badly done, it was wrong ;
it wanted more passion; forget the audience, and
throw yourself more into the part.' He used to
answer—' You are the only one who finds fault with
my acting.' ' Yes,' she would say, ' listen to me.
I will tell you when you have done very well, and
then you will see the difference;' and he waited
anxiously for the word of praise to make him happy.

My mother's ' Tu l'as très bien fait; bravo, Mario,'
gave him more pleasure than all the noise and din
of the public; and even when she had quitted the
stage, and my father, who was still singing, had new
rôles to study, she would go with him to the rehearsals and scold or praise him as if he were still
a *débutant.*"

Mrs. Godfrey Pearse and Mr. Willert Beale have
between them noted down more interesting particulars about Grisi and Mario than were ever
before recorded concerning any vocalist. Some intensely amusing anecdotes of artistic triumphs in
Dublin are given by both writers. Once, for instance,
when Grisi's admirers had dragged her carriage to
the hotel, and she had sung to them the " Minstrel
Boy," " as if she were tearing the harp strings
asunder, and singing from the depth of her heart,"
the enthusiasm of the people knew no bounds.
" They climbed up the lamp-post," says Mrs. Godfrey Pearse, " we thought they would have come
into the room, and when one speaker called out,
' Leave us one of your children,' our fright was
awful. In a chorus of pitiful little voices we begged
mamma not to leave us behind—we would be such
good children."

" It has been often said," remarks Mr. Willert
Beale, " and insisted upon, with perhaps more
earnestness than the point really deserves, that
Mario owed all his artistic training to Giulia Grisi.

According to some self-constituted authorities on the subject, he would never have been more than a tolerable *tenore leggiero* had it not been for the encouragement, example, and tuition he received from her. While admitting that Mario derived every advantage as a young artist from being associated with Donna Giulia during the first few years of his career, and that in all probability it was attributable to her guidance and instigation in those early days that he gradually lost all trace of being a 'stick of an actor,' I cannot help thinking that it was owing to his genius, or, at any rate, to his ambition, that they ultimately came to be acknowledged as the two greatest histrionic singers that ever trod the operatic stage. And I think so for this reason : they might with comparative ease and leisure have continued to appear together in the *Barbiere, Don Pasquale, Marta,* and similar works had he not looked higher in the sphere of lyric art, and determined that *Les Huguenots, Prophète, Favorita, Otello,* and other operas, demanding the highest development of dramatic as well as vocal skill and inspiration, should be added to their common *répertoire.* It is thus that a popular singer can aid and stimulate the progress of music, and it is beyond doubt that Mario used all the influence he had, at home and abroad, in the desirable direction indicated. As I can testify, he bestowed the most scrupulous care, study, and forethought upon the production of the operas in which he and Giulia Grisi might be concerned. No trouble was too great, no research too laborious to ensure any *rôles* they had undertaken being represented as historically correct and as perfectly as possible. He would rewrite a libretto if the version submitted to him did not meet with his approval. For instance, he rewrote every line of his part in Gounod's *Faust* because, he said, the original words of the Italian version were not sufficiently singable to please him. To those who have given no attention to the subject it may appear to be a matter of supreme indifference whether in words intended to be sung consonants, sibilants, or vowels predominate; whether the sentences chiefly commence and terminate with hard or soft letters. To Mario's sensitive ear and fastidious taste such points were of the utmost importance— as, indeed, they are—and he altered the versification of *Faust* and other operas accordingly. The copy of *Faust* in which he made the alterations is still extant. Strips of paper are pasted over the original text, and the words he substituted for the latter are very carefully written in upon the paper, under the notes as they occur.

"The volume in question is, together with his library of music, at Cagliari. I hope when these 'Recollections' are published in a complete form to be able to give his version of some of the words of *Faust*.

"As regards costume, no actor could be more particular than Mario as to what should be worn upon the stage, and he was as careful in the selection of costumes for Giulia Grisi as he was about his own. Cotton velvet was an object of special abhorrence to him. He used to declare that the touch of it was enough to give him an *attaque des nerfs*.

"In some of his engagements he would stipulate for a certain sum being allowed him for his dresses, in order that he might exercise his discretion in providing them. The amount agreed upon was almost always exceeded at his own expense, the costumier's bill being increased by the purchase of costly *bizarre* ornaments, perhaps very useless in the opinion of a manager, but indispensable from Mario's point of view to complete a living picture of the character he intended to impersonate.

"It is interesting to note how, in dressing for the stage, Mario anticipated, if he did not lead, some of the fashions of everyday life. To give height to his figure he wore heels so high that he practically walked on tiptoe. This revival of an old custom was generally followed, until high heels again became *rococo*, and on that account fell into disuse. The danger and inconvenience they involved had, of course, no weight whatever with those who wore them for fashion's sake. Mario discontinued them on retiring from the stage; they unquestionably gave him that particular jaunty walk by which he was so easily recognized. It was a suggestion of his to have side-springs made to boots, in order to afford the ankle more support than it has without such a contrivance. The springs were at first made of metal, and had such a clumsy appearance that they were laughed at and turned into ridicule. Mario, however, insisted upon ordering pair after pair, until at length his Paris bootmaker hit upon the brilliant notion of improving the metal springs, as an Irish servant might say, by making them of india-rubber. This met the difficulty of clumsiness, and put an end to turning into ridicule a suggestion which has ever since been universally adopted.

" When at the height of his popularity in Paris, a firm of Lyons silk manufacturers offered him a very large sum if he would set the fashion of silk coats and trousers. But Mario was no coxcomb and declined the offer. His dress in private was as simple as it could be, unless loose ruffles on wristbands and shirt-front be considered signs of dandyism. These he wore for many years, being of opinion that they are admissible in modern costume, as they break the otherwise harsh lines of male attire.

" He never wore jewellery of any description. If rings or other trinkets were given him, as, for example, in Russia, where it used to be the custom of the Court to make such presentations to the principal artists engaged at the Opera-house, St. Petersburg, the gifts invariably found their way to Donna Giulia's jewel case, and were ultimately converted into ornaments for her use. Giulia Grisi's collection of jewels was at one time of priceless value. The Diva sold a large portion of them to Silvani, formerly a well-known Brighton jeweller, and invested the proceeds in building a house in the Rue des Bassins, at that time a new street in Paris, near the Arc du Triomphe. I have good reason to remember a *châtelaine* she used to wear, suspended from which, with other baubles, was an old-fashioned gold watch, set with innumerable diamonds and other precious stones. We were at Ventnor when, after a stroll on the sands, upon returning to the hotel Donna Giulia discovered that she had lost this *châtelaine* together with all the valuables hanging to it. Great was the dismay caused by the discovery.

"'Are you sure you had it on when we went out?' asked Mario.

"'I think so, but am not quite certain,' was the reply.

"Search was then made in the hotel, and during the time thus lost we found upon going back to the beach that the rising tide had covered that part of the sands where we had been walking.

"'It will be washed away when the tide recedes,' remarked Ciabatta, who was one of the party.

"'Not with the sea as calm as it is at present,' replied Mario; 'the worst chance is that, being so heavy, it may sink into the sand. We must not lose sight of the spot where it may have fallen.' We waited some time watching the incoming tide, and then it was decided that Martin, Mario's valet, should be placed on guard while we went to dinner.

" A chair was brought; Martin was instructed to remain seated in it until we could renew our search. This was done in the evening by moonlight. Up and down the beach we walked, straining our eyes in vain.

" ' It has been washed away,' repeated Ciabatta.

" ' No!' insisted Mario, 'it has sunk into the sand.'

" And, luckily, he was right. We had given up all hope of ever seeing the missing *châtelaine* again, whether it had been washed away or was buried in oblivion by its own weight, when suddenly a bright speck glittered at our feet. It was one of the diamonds on the watch-case shining in the moonlight, and proved a guiding star to the hiding place of all its highly-prized companions.

"During the London season Grisi and Mario usually occupied a house on the banks of the Thames, preferring the tranquillity such a residence affords to the noise and bustle of town life, of which they met with sufficient to satisfy the most insatiable craving for such excitement when fulfilling their theatrical and other professional engagements. Moreover, to live away from the smoke of London was considered healthier for their children, whose welfare was the object of their unceasing attention and solicitude.

" For three seasons successively they lived at Mulgrave House, Fulham; then at Fairfax House, Putney; Gothic Lodge, Clapham Park; Arlington House, Turnham Green; and finally, during their last season, at Fernleigh, Leigham-Court Road, Streatham.

" Would you see them, as I can in memory, in the full enjoyment of domestic happiness? Come with me and we will call upon them at Mulgrave House, Fulham, one of their most favourite places of abode. It is a hot summer day in the middle of June. The sun pours down its fiercest rays from a cloudless sky, the trees are in full leaf, and the pleasant tepid air is fragrant with the perfume of the sweetest flowers. On our way to Fulham we see Hyde Park swarmed with fashionable life. Could we detect the subject of the buzz of conversation among the moving crowd of *flâneurs* it would probably prove to be Grisi and Mario at the Italian Opera the night before, for they are the talk of London, having just appeared in the *Huguenots* at the time you are about to be introduced to them. It is past mid-day when we reach Mulgrave House; the door is opened by an Italian servant, who receives us with a broad grin of welcome, and says that the Signora is in the garden but that the Signor has not yet come down to breakfast. We enter without further inquiry, and passing through the dining-room, from which daylight is carefully excluded by closely-drawn sun-blinds, we find Donna Giulia seated on the lawn under a spreading tree, watching the children at play around her. She wears a prodigiously large garden hat, which by no stretch of politeness can be called becoming ; and a snow-white summer costume, which certainly displays her glossy raven black hair and southern complexion to more advantage than the hat. She must know that nothing can impair the beauty of her expressive face, or surely she would never put on such head-gear. These, I dare say, are your thoughts as you behold the Diva, and I candidly confess I should quite agree with you if you expressed such an opinion aloud. Were you or I ungallant enough to venture to do so, it would be taken very good-naturedly, and we should be told with a kindly shrug of the shoulders that she never dressed for show, but always for comfort and convenience. We are received with radiant smiles, and I am very certain you will never forget those laughter-loving eyes that beam on you from under the far-reaching brim of the ugly hat—at least, if you do, you are less impressionable than any of your fellow creatures who have ever had the privilege of speaking to Giulia Grisi. 'Did you see Mario as you came through the house?' asks Donna Giulia, when the first words of greeting are over. We reply in the negative, and say that we believe he has not yet breakfasted.

"'It will be cold,' she exclaims, and making a hurried excuse she runs away from us across the lawn to go and see that the breakfast is properly attended to. I introduce you to the children and their governess, and we are invited to take part in a game at 'La Grâce,' in which we both distinguish ourselves, but each in a different way. You are declared an expert at the game, while I am laughed at as a decided failure. Presently Donna Giulia returns, saying, 'Mario will be with us in a few minutes.' She has half-a-dozen of those small red account books in her hand, and placing them on the garden seat explains to us that she has brought them from the kitchen, and that they are her weekly household accounts, which she has to examine and correct during the day. A prosaic duty you may think for 'Valentina' of the *Hugue-nots!*

"'Raoul' at length comes on to the lawn, of course smoking a cigar. I never knew him without one, and have seen him take a sponge bath with a lighted cigar in his mouth, while holding an enormous sponge with both hands over his head. There never was a more inveterate smoker. It did not matter what he had to smoke so long as it had any claim to be called tobacco. Not that he was indifferent to the quality of his cigars ; on the contrary, he always bought the very best to be obtained, but would put up with any kind rather than be deprived of his favourite luxury.

" ' How do you do ? Will you smoke ? ' he slowly exclaims, saluting us courteously and offering us his cigar-case, in very broken English, which he will continue to try and speak, out of compliment to you, unless you happen to be proficient in French or Italian.

" He is most plainly dressed, as I have already told you he would be—a slouch hat, loose shirt and necktie, shooting jacket and trousers completing his attire. He is, nevertheless, one of the most picturesque figures you ever saw ; his skin tawny with the sun, long dark eyelashes, thin, black, pointed beard, and exceptionally handsome features forming an *ensemble* as effective as any painter could dream of for a subject. He invites us to stay to lunch, and the invitation is repeated by Donna Giulia, but as you seem to think we have already exceeded the limits of a morning call, we decline, and assure them we must return to town.

" Mulgrave House was not accessible to all comers. It was beset by visitors, to some of whom it puzzled the servants to refuse admittance. The strangers that came were numberless. They were of all nationalities and of all classes, and made every possible excuse for calling. Some were wealthy and claimed the right of placing Mulgrave House on their visiting list by reason of their position in society; others were poor and sought relief there which they failed to find elsewhere. . . And of these latter a deserving case never went from the door empty-handed. The amount of money thus disbursed by Mario and Grisi must have been immense, although it was never known, for their alms were not recorded, being generally given with the understanding that their names should not be published. I say this from personal knowledge of facts that prove the statement. At different times when they were under engagement to me I have distributed for them in the aggregate a large sum, the amount thus paid away in charity to their order being made up of donations varying from one to a hundred pounds, and the recipients frequently being perfect strangers to the donors.

"I never knew of any application for assistance being made to them in vain, and can call to mind many instances in which the relief afforded by them was spontaneous and of a nature truly princely.

"Little time at Mulgrave House, or wherever else they might be residing, was devoted to music. Mario's favourite occupations at home were modelling in clay—in which pursuit he became an adept, and produced some really good work—and painting, of which as much cannot be said, although he persevered in it. He was, however, an accomplished draughtsman, and especially so of ornamental borders for mounting drawings. A design of his for a mount for Millais's picture of the 'Huguenot' is remarkable. A serpent is represented looking up into the picture, at the side of which is shown a monk peering out of a cell, threatening the Huguenot. Mario read deeply, antiquarian lore being the subject which possessed the greatest interest for him. His library of books on the topic was extensive, and his purchases of objects of so-called *bric-a-brac* were constant and innumerable. He was well known in Wardour Street as a most desirable customer. Donna Giulia's time at home was passed in attending to her household and her children. Business matters were, moreover, always looked after by her, and ratified by Mario when cheques or his signature to any other documents might be required.

" Away from the theatre they led a most tranquil life. Mario strongly objected to going into society, which he typified as the misery of putting on a white cravat. They were never happier than during an evening at home, when, after dinner, while Giulia Grisi would take some knitting in hand, Mario would walk up and down the room with a cigar, listening to his daughters' playing on the pianoforte such of Strauss' valses as he might select; now and again he would interrupt the amateur pianists to tell them the appropriate expression to be given to the different melodies, or he would ask them to choose some of Mozart's music while he amused himself with a game at ' Patience,' and in beating time to the music that happened to be played. ' Patience ' was Mario's only game at cards, for he was no card-player. Friends were received by Grisi and Mario with true hospitality, frankly and without ceremony.

Except on days when they had to sing they never denied themselves to those who had once had *entrée* to their house. Upon such occasions they much disliked seeing anyone. Throughout their career neither of them lost the nervousness each experienced in appearing before the public, and the nervousness was never overcome until after the first act of an opera. Donna Giulia invariably complained of hoarseness in the morning, and although I never knew her to break an engagement she always seemed to be on the point of doing so. They walked out generally alone, and dined early in the afternoon on opera days; at dinner, and indeed at all other times, they rarely, if ever, drank any other wine than claret, and of that very sparingly. Donna Giulia would sing a few scales for half-an-hour in the morning. Mario did not even indulge in that amount of vocal exercise. Ten minutes before starting for the theatre, while the servant would be waiting, watch in hand, assuring his master he would be late, was all the practice Mario thought necessary to keep his voice in order. That he required to exercise his voice so slightly was probably owing to the extreme delicacy and sensitiveness of his throat. This sensitiveness was evident in his susceptibility to the least change of temperature. I have been with him at the theatre when he has opened the window of his dressing-room on a hot summer night, and leant out to smoke a cigar. He was in capital voice and without the least trace of hoarseness. After smoking for a few minutes he became, while speaking, suddenly so husky as to be almost unable to continue the opera in which he was singing. He did so, however, to his great personal inconvenience rather than necessitate a change of programme and disappoint those who had come to hear him.

" New operas were studied with a professor, the assistance of Alary being in most instances secured for the purpose. This assistance was all the more necessary considering that neither Mario nor Grisi knew much, if anything, of the theory of music. Both could pick out a few chords on the pianoforte, Donna Giulia of the two being the more accomplished pianist. Her *répertoire* of instrumental music consisted mainly of Jullien's 'Original Polka' and the 'Tre Nozze Polka' by Alary, learned expressly for the recreation of the children.

"Although Mario may have been no musician so far as his fingers were concerned, yet he could give

hints of the greatest value to those who were or
who pretended to be.

" The art of accompanying, he used to say, is dis-
played in following, supporting, and aiding the
singer, not in hurrying him, nor in drowning his
voice.

"An accompanist, in his opinion, should never be
timid, but if uncertain of the notes to be played
should nevertheless strike firmly and courageously,
otherwise the singer gets confused, loses confi-
dence in himself and the accompaniment, and the
effect intended to be produced suffers irretrievably
in consequence.

" In studying any new composition, whether the
most important opera or the simplest ballad, they
followed a set plan. It was this : The words were
first considered, and when the intention and meaning of the text had been clearly ascertained and
fully understood, then, and not till then, the music
with which it was associated was learnt by heart,
every salient feature and opportunity for effect being
most carefully thought over and decided upon. It
was one of Mario's maxims that unless a singer had
all that he was singing about thoroughly in his head
as well as in his throat he could never do himself
justice; ' but,' he used to say, ' if you get as
familiar as you should be with your work, then,
when you are in the humour and in good voice, you
can let yourself go with the certainty almost of pro-

ducing the effect you intend upon your audience, that is to say, if you ever have any moments of inspiration.

" I have heard Meyerbeer discuss the libretto of the *Huguenots* with Grisi and Mario, and I may say, without, I hope, being thought presumptuous in saying it, that I have assisted both of them in study-ing many of the English songs they sang, and, whether considering the dramatic effects to be made by ' Raoul ' and ' Valentina,' or in taking in hand ' Good-bye, Sweetheart,' or ' The Minstrel Boy,' the plan they followed was the same: the words were thought of first, then the music, and with the words and music combined particular attention was given to the points to be dwelt upon and made pro-minent. These latter were not allowed to be too frequent, but were so chosen as to make the deepest impression. The importance of such a plan as this can hardly be over-rated. It seems not only to ensure singing with intelligence, but to save a singer very much unnecessary exertion by marking down the intervals where energy has to be used as well as those where the voice may, so to speak, be nursed and kept in reserve.

" Such a system of study was indispensable to Giulia Grisi, who was one of the most impulsive singers ever known. Had her genius not been sub-ject to some control it would have run riot, and its fortunate possessor would have been its victim rather than its lovely exponent. Thus in 'Norma' this control was wanting to some extent, and the scenes with 'Pollio' were thought by many to be too violent, although taken as a whole her performance of the part was one of transcendent dignity and grandeur. In the trio 'Trema o vil' it was often remarked that the fury of the Diva was exaggerated, and appeared to threaten the total annihilation of the faithless 'Pollio.' A simple-minded tenor, Albicini by name, once came to me while he was performing 'Pollio' to Giulia Grisi's 'Norma,' and with tears in his eyes declared he could not go on the stage again after the storm of rage and passion he had encountered in the trio scene.

" 'La Signora shook her fist at me and treated me like a dog,' he said, nearly choked with emotion. In order to pacify him, I took him to the Diva's dressing-room, and when I had explained how matters stood all his trouble ended in a burst of hearty laughter and reassurance from the High Priestess herself.

" I am justified in believing that it was owing to Mario's view of this particular scene and to his gallant reluctance to suggest any modification of it that he so decidedly objected to the *rôle* of 'Pollio.' He never sang it unless asked to do so as a special favour to his impresario. In spite of her impulsiveness on the stage, Giulia Grisi undoubtedly improved her rendering of different characters by practical experience and by the advice of Mario. Such was notably the case in the *Trovatore*, a work they studied together long after the Diva's reading of 'Norma' had become too confirmed for any alteration to be suggested in it. In the 'Miserere' scene of the *Trovatore* 'Leonora' recognizes 'Manrico's' voice, and all soprani representing the part when the opera was first introduced were in the habit of standing before the footlights and singing 'Leonora's' music facing the audience, with no more heed for the dramatic nature of the situation than if they had been singing in a concert-room. Donna Giulia followed the custom of her predecessors and came down to the footlights in the ' Miserere ' the first time she appeared as ' Leonora.' But on the second occasion a remarkable change was noticeable. The heroine was observed to display more action in the scene than had ever before been exhibited. ' Leonora' wandered round the stage in despair, as though really seeking to discover from which part of the prison walls the voice of her lover proceeded. She clung to the tower and sang the thrilling passages in answer to ' Manrico' with gestures and expression which kept the spectators spell-bound.

"'Ah ! Che la Morte' had never before created such a sensation as it did that evening, and it was ' Leonora's ' intensely dramatic action that added to its effect and contributed to its enhanced success. Since then Giulia Grisi's rendering of the 'Miserere' scene has always been adopted, although I dare say very few may know by whom it was originated.

"'Your English stage,' said Mario to me on one occasion when we were speaking of the production of a new opera at Covent Garden, 'your English stage affords a striking contrast to that of the French.'

"'In what respect?' I inquired, anxious to hear his opinion on the subject.

"'In having no recognized school of acting,' he replied; and continued the conversation very much as follows: 'You have no school so called, but there is more individuality among your actors than the Frenchmen display. The latter are slaves to their school, which imparts a stiffness and conventionality to their dramatic delivery and action. They have a style for tragedy and a style for comedy, with rigid rules for each, and but little, if any, variety in either. If at all familiar with the French school of acting, you can tell the reading—the very gestures—that will be given to any particular part by any disciple of the school, so strict are the rules laid down and so scrupulously are they obeyed. Occasionally the genius of an actor will force him or her to break through the firmly established conventionalities and strike out a new path. That is, however, very much

more rarely the case on the French than on the
English stage, where, as far as I have been able to
observe, individuality takes the place of a school.
For instance, to illustrate my meaning, a Macready
appears upon your stage and immediately he is set
up as the model to be copied in tragedy, and he has
accordingly a crowd of followers. I admire Macready as an artist devoted to his art immensely, but
I differ with him in his view of some of the characters I have seen him represent. His " Othello," for
example, is much too savage throughout—his black
looks, growling voice, harsh and repulsive manner,
would render it impossible for any " Desdemona,"
however susceptible, to fall in love with him.
" Othello," to my mind, in the earlier scenes of the
play at any rate, should be shown as an irresistibly
attractive man to womankind, in order to account
for " Desdemona's " passion and undoubted devotion
to him. Macready makes him a murderer from the
very commencement, and anticipates the tragic scene
in Act V. by almost every look, tone of voice, and
gesture.'

" ' It is Macready's style of tragedy,' I observed.
' It is said that he growled so loudly and looked so
like a savage during one of the performances at
Windsor Castle that the Royal children were fright-
ened and began to cry.'

" ' That is a bit of humorous satire,' replied Mario.
' Of course Macready may justify his reading of

"Othello," and has, I daresay, devoted a good deal of study to it. He must have done so, and I should be glad to have an opportunity of discussing it with him, for in the details I have referred to I should certainly venture to ask him why he makes the Moor so unnatural. Human nature, after all, must be our guide in all dramatic representations; and if the "Othello" of Macready would be repellent to a woman as a lover in real life, it must be just as much so upon the stage, and Macready's reading of the part is therefore open to objection.'

"Here is another interesting specimen of Signor Mario's conversation on æsthetic subjects. After repeating his observation that in English acting there was no school, and that our dramatic artists modelled their style upon that of the leading actors who had made the most impression upon them, he added that the danger in such a system was 'that the stage may be pervaded by individualities and that the models may be too servilely copied.' But, continued Mario, 'that is a danger common to every branch of art, and is only averted by copyists gaining experience, and at last learning to think and work for themselves, becoming in their turn models for those who follow in their footsteps. The affinity of the arts is really very close. Take the obstacle which it is so difficult for all young actors to conquer, that of restlessness. I remember well when it was as impossible for me to stand still upon the stage as it was to know what to do with my arms and legs when before the public. And in music, painting, literature, all the arts, in fact, restlessness is a chief difficulty to be overcome by every beginner. The compositions of a young musician are generally full of abstruse modulations, as though a change of key were the greatest effect to be achieved in music; the efforts of a youthful painter are almost invariably wanting in the repose which experience alone can give; the poet, dramatist, and *littérateur* in their early works are never content without constant change of scene. And as the actor who has overcome restlessness upon the stage may be said to have made some progress in his vocation, so may the composer, painter, writer, and every other follower of art be satisfied that he has studied to some good purpose when he has become convinced of the necessity of expressing his thoughts by the simplest means, and is able to do so with the least exertion.' "

Mr. Willert Beale, son of Mr. Beale (of the firm of Cramer, Beale, and Co.), under whose management the Royal Italian Opera was founded, will some day, it must be hoped, write the lives of Mario and Grisi, which would naturally involve a history of Italian Opera during its most flourishing period, from 1828, when Madame Grisi made her *début* at Bologna as " Emma" in Rossini's *Zelmira*, to 1871, when Mario, as " Fer-

nando" in *La Favorita,* took his farewell of the stage.
From the time when the Royal Italian Opera was
opened Mr. Willert Beale was for many years in
constant relations with the illustrious operatic pair;
and he enjoys, moreover, the advantage of having
been permitted to make at will copious extracts
from the highly interesting book of recollections
written by one of their daughters, Mrs. Godfrey
Pearse, and still, for the most part, in MS.   Mr.
Willert Beale having, with the greatest kindness,
placed, in his turn, at my disposition both his own
personal recollections and his extracts from Mrs.
Godfrey Pearse's diary, I have drawn freely from
both sources; though far less freely than I should
have done had I not felt convinced that Mr. Willert
Beale would, some day, turn to account, in the
manner above suggested, his abundant knowledge,
direct and communicated, of the most gifted and
most accomplished operatic couple that ever lived.

  "Both my father and mother were supposed to be
taller than they really were," writes Mrs. Godfrey
Pearse, in the book of recollections just referred to,
"the stage giving that effect; my mother was a little
over five feet two inches, my father five feet nine.
They both held themselves remarkably erect.   My
mother was almost haughty in her movements, and
had a stately way of walking which suited her
queenly head.   Her features were small and Grecian
in character, with a soft pale complexion.   When on

the stage she used only powder, never any paint.
Her eyes were blue, with raven black hair, eyelashes,
and eyebrows. Her greatest beauty was, however,
in her smile and expression. How well we, her
children, remember its soft and gentle look! Her
love for her children was beyond all words to con-
vey. She had six girls, of whom she lost three.
The death of her little ones caused her grief to which
she almost succumbed. The eldest, Giulietta, died
at the tender age of eighteen months, in Paris; this
child was the idol of her parents, and her early loss
almost broke their hearts. Moreover, she died only
a few days before the date fixed for my mother's
benefit and first appearance in a new opera—a
double event to which all Paris was looking forward. It was impossible to disappoint the public,
and with an aching heart my poor mother betook
herself to her duty, and never fulfilled it better.
The enthusiasm of the artist conquered, for the time,
the anguish of the mother, and she surpassed herself. The audience were as enthusiastic in their
turn, and overwhelmed her with plaudits, and more
than the usual floral tributes of admiration. Next
morning the idol of the night before waited at the
gate of Père la Chaise until it was opened, that she
might be the first to enter the cemetery and lay
the results of her triumph on her little darling's
grave.

"Her next loss was that of Angelina, who also died

in Paris, of croup, when little more than two years of age. I was a baby six months old at the time, and when my little sister died I am told my mother was frantic with sorrow to find me exhibiting symptoms of croup. In despair she snatched me up, and, rushing out of the house, insisted upon being conveyed to England, the country always most dear to her, feeling convinced that once over here she would have a chance of saving me. Heedless of my father's remonstrances, she started, and landing at Dover, after a long and fatiguing journey, with her baby clasped to her bosom, arrived at the Lord Warden Hotel, beseeching those who met her to save her child. The hostess, a motherly, kind woman, promptly soothed her agitation by immediately attending to the sick baby, putting her into a warm bath and doing all she possibly could. The croup gradually got worse and my poor mother's anxiety increased. I was, however, at length declared out of danger, and my mother was ever after superstitiously convinced that if I had been allowed to remain in Paris my resting place would have been near that of Giulietta in Père la Chaise.

"The third loss my parents sustained was that of Bella Maria, their youngest child, who died at Brighton when four years old, after a lingering illness of six months, borne with angelic patience by the poor little sufferer. My mother had moved from place to place, hoping that change of air would do good, and after her performances would bring her wreaths and bouquets to Bella, longing to see the little one smile. She never recovered this loss, and before her own death her last words were to call for her child Bella; they now lie side by side. How little did the public know of my mother's grief at this time when they heard her singing to their delight; but I shall never forget how she suffered! When she appeared for the first time after Bella's death, in *Norma*, in the scene where ' Norma' rushes to stab the two sleeping children, one of the latter, with its curly black hair, suddenly brought back the remembrance of the loss she had sustained, and she broke down; flinging the dagger aside, my mother threw herself over the two little stagers and sobbed aloud, as though her heart would break."

Mario was equally attached to his children. He seems to have had no pleasures apart from his family; and he hated going into society. He possessed many artistic accomplishments; and Mr. Beale has told us that he modelled well in clay, and, without being much of a painter, was a good draughtsman. He had a taste, too, for ornamental work; and some of his designs for picture frames showed fancy as well as ingenuity. Often he would rewrite the words of his operatic part; for, apart from all theory on the subject, he found it impossible to give dramatic expression to words that were meaningless.

Mario was temperate, almost to abstemiousness, as regards wine, but smoked to excess—or, at least, perpetually. Sir Morell Mackenzie may be interested to hear that he avoided cigarettes, holding that the fumes from the paper irritated the throat; an opinion which I have been told on good authority is entertained generally by the physicians of Eastern Europe. Mario smoked the first thing in the morning in his bath and the last thing at night in his bed. He smoked behind the scenes when engaged in a representation; and, in contravention of the law, he smoked in the streets of St. Petersburg. Meeting him one day on the Nevsky Prospect, and pretending not to see that he held a lighted cigar up his sleeve, the Emperor Nicholas occupied him in conversation, and went on talking until at last Mario's sleeve took fire. "Vous brûlez, Monsieur Mario!" exclaimed the Tsar. Then, much amused by the incident, he gave him full permission to smoke when and where he pleased.

Both Grisi and Mario had a superstitious horror of enterprises begun on a Friday and of the number thirteen in connection with all matters. What, then, must have been the effect of Friday and thirteen in combination?

Sir Julius Benedict once told me that after succeeding, with great difficulty, in persuading Mario to sing on a Thursday evening at a house in Belgrave Square he felt it necessary to conceal from him the fact that the number of the house was thirteen. But Mario noticed it when, late on Thursday night, after a performance at the Royal Italian Opera, they arrived together at their destination. To make the matter worse, a neighbouring church clock, just as the carriage drove up, struck twelve. It was midnight—Friday, that is to say, had already begun; and to sing for the first time on a Friday at a house numbered thirteen was more than Mario cared to do. In spite of Benedict's arguments and representations he insisted upon being driven home.

Mr. Willert Beale declares that both Grisi and Mario so dreaded the fatal number that they shrank even from mentioning it by name. Vain would it have been to reason with them on the subject, for it so happened that they had an array of facts to support their view. " Some of the instances," says Mr. Willert Beale, " were curious enough, and might puzzle Quetelet himself to account for. . . . I remember when Mario returned from Paris, whither he had gone with the remains of their child who died at Brighton, to place them in the grave at Père la Chaise, he told me he had been pursued by the number which he would never mention if he could possibly avoid doing so throughout the melancholy journey. He was delayed on the road, and arrived in Paris on the thirteenth day of the month, the carriage in which he travelled and the cabin he occupied on board the steamer were numbered with the same

ominous figures, and when the case accompanying
him came to be unpacked a large card inscribed with
No. 13 was found nailed to the exterior of the coffin
the case contained. I have known Mario efface the
number whenever it has occurred—on the doors of
an hotel, for instance—in order that it should not
meet the gaze of Donna Giulia."

Grisi, whether by keeping clear of number thirteen and by declining to begin any new enterprise
on a Friday, or from other causes, is said to have
been lucky herself (she had indeed been fortunately
endowed by nature) and to have brought good luck
to all connected with her. Prosperity attended her,
even to the end of her first series of farewell performances. But she tempted Fate. Not content
with having sung, ostensibly for the last time, and
with the most brilliant success, her principal parts
with " Norma," " Lucrezia Borgia," " Valentine "
and " Donna Anna " among them, she arranged to
take leave of the public once more. Thus she
had two farewells ; the first at the Royal Italian
Opera, in the summer of 1861 ; the second soon
afterwards, at Her Majesty's Theatre.

Mario continued after Grisi's retirement to sing
for many years ; and it was not until her death in
1869 that he resolved to leave the stage.

He was at St. Petersburg fulfilling an engagement when suddenly he was informed that he
must start at once for the Prussian capital. The

news of Grisi's death had been telegraphed to the director of the Imperial Opera-house, and by him communicated to the Emperor. With characteristic kindness, Alexander II. sent for Mario and, liberating him from his engagement, told him to take the train without delay for Berlin, as "sad intelligence had been telegraphed concerning Madame Grisi." Mario was completely staggered by the news. Leaving the Emperor's presence, he started at once for the railway station.

" Ne me dites pas qu'elle est morte!" he exclaimed to the friends around him ; and it was not until he reached Berlin that the " sad intelligence " in its full significance became known to him. " He sank down on the sofa in the drawing-room," writes his daughter, "and wept like a child. We three were sleeping in the room adjoining, and his sobs woke us up. We called him to come and embrace us, and we mingled our tears with his. His agony of mind seemed to be increased by the reflection that, after more than thirty years passed by her side, he had not been with her during her last moments."

Mario now left the stage as soon as he could complete his engagements; giving a series of farewell representations at the St. Petersburg Opera-house in 1870, and at the Royal Italian Opera of London in 1871. He made his last appearance at the age of 61 as " Fernando " in *La Favorita;* and never did he sing or act more superbly than at his final performance.

Thirteen years later Mr. W. G. Cusins, passing through Rome, called on Mario and found him in a dying condition. As he was waiting to be admitted to the sick man's bed-chamber he noticed on the wall a full-size portrait of Grisi. The only other pictures were portraits of Mario's father and mother. "We shook hands," wrote Mr. Cusins, soon afterwards. "His first inquiry was after Her Majesty the Queen. He spoke with gratitude of the Queen and of the English nation generally; and I felt that my visit as an Englishman gave him intense pleasure in what he knew to be his last moments."

Two hours afterwards Mario was no more. Mr. Cusins telegraphed news of the sad event to Windsor, and received from one of the Queen's secretaries the following reply :—"Her Majesty, with sincere regret, has heard of Signor Mario's death, and desires you, if possible, to assist at his funeral, and place a wreath on his grave in the Queen's name."

Her Majesty's wishes were duly fulfilled.

END OF FIRST VOLUME.

INDEX TO NAMES.

A.

B.

C.

F.

G.

H.

Habeneck, 179.
Halévy, 66, 68, 240.
Hallmandel, M., 244.
Handel, 8, 14, 18, 22, 23, 30, 43, 44, 47, 49, 50, 54, 66, 76, 118, 177, 212, 213, 245.
Harrington, Countess of, 234.
Harrington, Dr., 115.
Harris, Augustus, 167.
Hasse, 52, 53, 54, 76, 118.
Hawkins, 25.
Haym, Nicolo, 8, 14, 21.
Heine, 222, 274.

Heinel, 109.
Helvetius, 100.
Hemstoff (Hermstorff), 218.
Henry IV., 102.
d'Hennin, Prince, 88, 89, 90.
Herring, Dr. Thomas, 36, 37.
Hertford, Lord, 232.
Hill, Aaron, 23.
Hiller, 116, 156, 179, 180, 185.
Holtei, Karl von, 219, 220, 221.
Houldin, 104.
Houssaye, M. Arséne, 107.

J.

Jahn, Otto, 91.
Jarente, Monseigneur de, 99.
Jettel, 216, 232.

Joseph, Emperor, 77, 121.
Junot, General, 126.

K.

Karr, Alphonse, 59.
Klingemann, 248, 249.

Knyvett, 249.

L.

Lablache, 201, 247, [251, 274.
Lago, Signor, 167.
Laguerre, Mdlle., 96, 97, 98, 102.
Lalouette, 67.
Lamballe, Princess de, 86.
Larrivée, 87.
Lauenstein, Mdlle. von, 234.
Lauragais, Count de, 89, 90, 102, 103, 104, 110, 111.
Lauragais, Chevalier de, 101.
Lauragais, Countess de, 103.
Lawes, 7.
Lawrence, 10.
Le Sage, 220.

Lemière-Desarges, Madame, 225.
Lesueur, Mdlle., 98.
Lewis, Mr., 34.
Lichfield, Lady, 42.
Liebic, 215.
Liegnitz, Princess, 226, 227.
Lieven, Countess, 184.
Lieven, Count, 183, 184.
Lind, Jenny, 190, 240.
Lipinsky, 250.
Liszt, 148.
Lock, 7.
Locke, 100.
Lockit, 35.
Loder, Mr., 128.
Lotte, 189.

Silvani, 282.
Sinclair, 181.
Smart, Sir George, 249.
Smith, Signor, 149, 153.
Smith, Joseph, 19.
Sontag, Franz Anton, 215.
Sontag, Henriette, 51, 112, 133, 182, 199, 213, 214, 215, 216, 217, 218, 219, 220, 221, 222, 224, 225, 226, 227, 228, 229, 230, 231, 232, 233, 234, 235, 236, 237, 239, 240, 241, 242.

Soubise, Prince de, 107.
Spohr, 230.
Stanhope, Lord (afterwards Lord Chesterfield), 25.
Steele, 21, 22.
Stendhal, 145, 152, 161, 176, 177, 194, 206.
Stephens, Miss, 234.
St. John, Florence, 27.
Stradella, 5.
Sully, 102.
Swift, 9, 18, 28, 31, 32, 34, 35, 36, 37, 38, 39, 40, 41.

T.

Taglioni, 188.
Tamberlik, 208.
Tamburini, 274.
Tennison, Dr. (afterwards Archbishop), 4.
Thalberg, Herr, 238, 239, 248, 249.
Thévenard, 71.
Thomas, Ambroise, 203.
Thurlow, Lady, 234.

Titiens, 182, 201, 204, 209.
Todi, Madame, 124, 213.
Tofts, Mrs., 8, 9, 10, 12, 13, 16, 18, 19, 20, 21, 22, 23, 47.
Traetta, 177.
Tramezzani, 127.
Trebelli, 182.
Troupenas, 260.
Tulou, 134.

U.

Urban VIII., 7.

V.

Vaccai, 192.
Valentini, Signor, 9, 21.
Valentini, Regina, 53, 54.
Valabrèque, M. de., 126, 137, 168.
Vanburgh, Sir John, 9.
Vaneschi, 55.
Vaughan, 249.
Visconti, Marquis, 42.

Velluti, 198.
Vento, 63.
Verdi, 146, 202, 203.
Verdier, Mdlle., 70.
Vernhagen, 225.
Véron, Dr., 140.
Vestris, 99, 192, 197.
Voltaire, 100, 101.

W.

Wagner, 158, 203, 214, 254.
Wagner, Johanna, 191.

Walker, Mr. Robert, 29.
Wallace, 256.

INDEX TO OPERAS AND ORATORIOS.